FROM THE FILMS OF

Harry Potter

AFTERNOON
TEA MAGIC

FROM THE FILMS OF

Harry Potter

AFTERNOON TEA MAGIC

OFFICIAL SNACKS, SIPS, AND SWEETS
INSPIRED BY THE WIZARDING WORLD

INCLUDES
CONTENT FROM

Text by Jody Revenson
Recipes by Veronica Hinke

INSIGHT
EDITIONS

SAN RAFAEL · LOS ANGELES · LONDON

CONTENTS

125 + CHAPTER THREE:

TEATIME CANDIES, SNACKS, AND TAKE-HOME GIFTS

145 + CHAPTER FOUR:

TEATIME TIPPLES, HOT DRINKS, AND MAGICAL MIXES

INTRODUCTION

The Harry Potter films are quintessentially British—with an all-British cast at Hogwarts and Hogsmeade, all-British locations, and even British nomenclature. Ginny wears a jumper (sweater), Harry wears trainers (sneakers), and there are Christmas crackers at every holiday celebration. And Luna Lovegood even hopes there will be pudding at the end-of-year feast—pudding being synonymous with desserts in Britain.

In the Fantastic Beasts films, Englishman Newt Scamander travels to various cities on different continents. In Paris, his Niffler, Teddy, who has a penchant for shiny objects, liberates an important item from Gellert Grindelwald, which Newt passes to his friend and mentor, Albus Dumbledore, upon their return to Hogwarts. Dumbledore in turn offers the Niffler tea as a reward. (Newt suggests just milk instead and reminds Dumbledore to hide the teaspoons.)

Perhaps there is nothing more iconically British than an afternoon tea, served on a three-tiered china tray laden with scrumptious confections and savory offerings. But how did the afternoon tea come about?

Afternoon tea evolved from the time of Queen Victoria and her ladies-in-waiting, who felt a bit hungry in the late afternoon, and began taking tea and small, light foods such as breads or biscuits (cookies). This became a daily gathering to share gossip and news and relax with friends. As the tea would be served on low tables in the queen's parlor, the get-together was called a "low" tea.

There is also a "high tea" that includes meats and a "cream tea" with tea and scones. Finally, there's a "royal tea" that includes champagne or sherry (or any type of alcohol these days). A typical tea service consists of a set of cups and saucers, small plates, and a teapot, sugar bowl, and milk pitcher.

The "proper" way to stir tea is back and forth, not in a circle. Shockingly, Professor Dolores Umbridge does not follow this rule when she stirs the pink sugar into her cup with a circular motion.

This deluxe cookbook offers recipes for nibbles, sweets, and brews that the seventh Duchess of Bedford would welcome warmly at her parlor gatherings. And you won't need Divination professor Sybill Trelawney to read your tea leaves to predict how much you and your guests will enjoy the magic of a Harry Potter–inspired afternoon tea.

CHAPTER ONE

SWEET FINGER TREATS AND SUGARY NIBBLES

"FUDGE HAS TO SEE BUCKBEAK
BEFORE WE STEAL HIM—
OTHERWISE HE'LL THINK
HAGRID SET HIM FREE."

—Hermione Granger
to Harry Potter

*Harry Potter and
the Prisoner of Azkaban*

HAGRID'S PUMPKIN TEATIME MADELEINES

Hagrid's pumpkin patch, created for *Harry Potter and the Prisoner of Azkaban*, provided a place for his Hippogriff, Buckbeak, to rest before the creature's execution—and for Buckbeak to be saved by Harry and Hermione when she uses the Time-Turner for his rescue. The molds for the smaller pumpkins were used again to create pumpkin-shaped chocolate cakes for the dessert feast in *Harry Potter and the Goblet of Fire*.

These custard-based teatime cakes use a classic madeleine recipe with a twist inspired by Hagrid's pumpkin patch. After the pumpkin-cinnamon-flavored madeleines bake, they're sprinkled lightly with powdered sugar. And they're the perfect size for a high tea bite.

½ cup plus
1 tablespoon butter,
melted and cooled,
divided

1 cup plus 1 tablespoon
all-purpose flour,
divided

2 large eggs

¾ cup granulated sugar

½ cup pumpkin pie
filling

1 teaspoon ground
cinnamon

½ teaspoon cardamom

½ teaspoon nutmeg

Pinch salt

1 tablespoon powdered
sugar

SPECIALTY TOOLS

Madeleine pan

Preheat the oven to 375°F.

Using 1 tablespoon of the melted butter, coat each individual cavity in the madeleine pan with butter. Make sure to coat crevices and indentations well. Use your fingers to sprinkle 1 tablespoon flour to lightly flour each mold.

In a large mixing bowl, beat the eggs and granulated sugar on low speed until combined well.

Add in the pumpkin, cinnamon, cardamom, nutmeg, and salt. Add the remaining 1 cup flour, followed by the remaining ½ cup butter. Stir with a mixing spoon just until thoroughly combined.

Fill each individual cavity of the madeleine pan with 2 tablespoons batter. Place in the oven and bake until lightly browned on the edges, 15 to 20 minutes.

Remove the madeleines from the oven and set them on a wire rack to cool while they are still in their molds. When the madeleines are cool, sprinkle each one with powdered sugar.

Store in an airtight container at room temperature for 3 to 4 days.

JACOB KOWALSKI'S
MINI TEATIME PACZKI

Paczki (the singular form being paczek) are bite-size, deep-fried, sugar-coated pillowy Polish doughnuts. When No-Maj Jacob Kowalski visits the Steen National Bank in New York to ask for a bank loan to open his own bakery in *Fantastic Beasts and Where to Find Them*, he proudly opens a suitcase with a selection of his homemade pastries to show the bank manager, including paczki based on his grandmother's recipe.

Actor Dan Fogler, who portrays Jacob Kowalski, has a reason for thinking it was kismet he played the part of a baker for the film. "I knew the character really well, because my grandfather was a baker," Fogler explains. "He had the best pumpernickel in New York; that's what he was known for."

Traditionally, paczki are jam-packed with a sweet prune filling, but there are endless varieties to choose from, such as lemon curd, apples, raspberries, or custard. These are filled with a honey-sweetened rum raisin compote.

FOR THE RUM RAISIN FILLING

3 cups raisins

2 cups dark spiced rum

½ cup honey

TO MAKE THE RUM RAISIN FILLING

In a medium bowl, combine the raisins and rum, and let sit in an airtight container in the refrigerator for at least 1 hour or overnight.

In a small kettle or saucepan on the stovetop over high heat, bring the raisin mixture and honey to a boil. Boil, stirring continuously, until the mixture thickens to the consistency of a fruit jam, about 4 to 5 minutes. Remove from heat and set aside, uncovered, until the filling cools, about 1 hour.

CONTINUED ON PAGE 16

"YOU GOTTA TRY THE
PACZKI. OKAY. IT'S MY
GRANDMOTHER'S RECIPE.
THE ORANGE ZEST.
JUST . . . (SIGHS)"

—Jacob Kowalski

*Fantastic Beasts and
Where to Find Them*

CONTINUED FROM PAGE 15

FOR THE PACZKI

3 cups all-purpose
flour, plus 2 cups
more for surfaces

¼ cup granulated sugar

¼ ounce active dry
yeast (1 packet)

½ teaspoon salt

¾ cup whole milk

¼ cup shortening

2 small eggs, room
temperature

¼ teaspoon white rum

Two 40-ounce
containers
vegetable oil

SPECIALTY TOOLS

Candy thermometer

TO MAKE THE PACZKI

In the bowl of a stand mixer with the dough hook attachment, combine 2 cups of the flour, the sugar, yeast, and salt.

In a medium saucepan over medium heat, combine the milk, shortening, and ¼ cup water until the mixture reaches 125°F on a candy thermometer. Remove the mixture from the heat as soon as it reaches 125°F. If the milk mixture is hotter than 125°F, it will affect the yeast when it is combined with the flour and yeast mixture.

Add the milk mixture to the bowl of the stand mixer with the flour mixture. Mix everything together well, beating at medium speed for 1 minute. Stop to scrape the flour from the sides of the bowl into the dough mixture. Add 1 cup flour and beat for another minute. Add the eggs, and beat into the mixture for 1 minute. Add the rum and beat it into the mixture for 1 minute. The dough will be wet and very sticky.

Sprinkle 1 cup of flour on the countertop. Knead the dough for 5 minutes. This step is very important. Kneading the dough helps distribute the yeast throughout. To knead the dough, use the palms of your hands to push the dough down on the countertop again and again, folding it over each time. Use the front or back of your hands. Keep pushing and folding repeatedly. If there is flour around the edges of your workspace, try to incorporate as little as possible into the dough as you knead.

Pour the 2 bottles of oil into the Dutch oven and then pour the remainder of one of the bottles (about ¼ teaspoon) into a large mixing bowl. Form the dough into a ball and place the dough in the bowl.

Turn the dough over so that both sides are covered with the oil. Cover the bowl with a towel, and set it aside in a warm, dry place away from windows or a frequently opened refrigerator; or near a warm stove, where the dough can rise for 1 hour. Try to avoid air-conditioning. The dough will not rise much; however, it will rise a little.

On the countertop where you kneaded the dough, spread the remaining 1 cup flour around to create a space to roll out the dough and cut it into round shapes. After 1 hour of resting, place the dough on the floured countertop. Push your fist into the dough to remove the air caused by the yeast and rising.

Use a rolling pin to roll out the dough to ½-inch thickness. Use a biscuit cutter or a 2- or 3-inch-round cookie cutter to cut out pieces of the dough. Set the pieces of dough on the counter, covered by a towel, to rise again, about 1 hour. The dough will not rise noticeably but will rise a little, which is enough.

While the dough is rising, heat the oil in the Dutch oven to 375°F. Use the candy thermometer to monitor the temperature. It is very important not to exceed 375°F. If the oil is too hot, the dough can burn before the paczki are cooked all the way through.

Place 3 or 4 pieces of dough at a time in the Dutch oven, frying them until they are golden brown all around on the outside, 1 to 2 minutes on each side.

Use a spider to pull each of the paczki out and set them on a plate lined with paper towels.

When the paczki and the rum raisin filling have cooled enough to touch, fill the paczki with the rum raisin filling. Fill a pastry bag with the rum raisin filling. Use a knife to poke a hole in the top of each paczek, and use the pastry bag to squeeze about 1 tablespoon of the filling into each of the paczki.

Store at room temperature in an airtight container for 2 to 3 days.

> "... THAT'S WHY I WANT TO MAKE PASTRIES. YOU KNOW. IT MAKES PEOPLE HAPPY."
>
> —Jacob Kowalski
>
> *Fantastic Beasts and Where to Find Them*

HOGWARTS HIGH TABLE ROASTED APPLE SCONE BITES WITH FRESH CREAM AND MINT

There were many feasts of main courses served in the Great Hall throughout the Harry Potter films, especially the Hogwarts welcome feast. So, set decorator Stephenie McMillan tried something new when welcoming the visiting students from Durmstrang and Beauxbatons for the Triwizard Tournament in *Harry Potter and the Goblet of Fire*: a dessert feast. Some of these puddings were completely edible, and others were not, depending on what could stay fresh under the hot movie lights.

Scones were a must at Queen Victoria's afternoon teatimes and would have been a perfect addition to the Triwizard Tournament welcome feast (and they wouldn't melt under the lights!). This bite-size take on the larger classic adds even more flavor into the feast, filled with roasted apples, cut into the shape of pie slices, and topped with a sprig of fresh mint.

FOR THE APPLE MIXTURE

1 cup fresh apples, peeled and chopped into ½-inch pieces

¼ cup light brown sugar

Juice from ½ lemon

¼ cup butter

FOR THE SCONE BATTER

3 cups all-purpose flour, plus more for rolling the dough on the counter

3 teaspoons baking powder

½ teaspoon baking soda

½ teaspoon salt

1 cup butter, cut into small pieces

1 egg

1 cup plain yogurt

½ teaspoon vanilla extract

2 teaspoons milk

1 teaspoon coarse sugar crystals, for sprinkling on top of the scones

FOR THE FRESH CREAM TOPPING

2 cups heavy whipping cream

½ cup granulated sugar

¼ teaspoon fresh lemon juice

FOR THE GARNISH

6 to 8 sprigs fresh pineapple mint

✦ BEHIND THE MAGIC ✦

Among Stephenie McMillan's favorite sweets were the ice mice and the chocolate rabbits that leaped out of top hat cakes.

TO MAKE THE APPLE MIXTURE

Preheat the oven to 400°F. In a large mixing bowl, toss the apples in the brown sugar and lemon juice. Let sit for at least 1 hour.

Place the apples in a skillet in the oven with the butter until softened and browned around the edges, 15 to 20 minutes. Stir every 5 minutes.

Remove the apples from the oven and let sit on the countertop until cooled to room temperature.

TO MAKE THE SCONE BATTER

In a large mixing bowl, combine the flour, baking powder, baking soda, and salt. Add the butter, and use your hands to mix everything together until it turns to coarse crumbs. Add the egg, yogurt, and vanilla, and continue to mix together until combined well.

When the roasted apples have cooled, add the apple mixture to the batter. Save ¾ cup apple mixture to place a dab on top of each scone when they are served. Knead the dough 4 times to incorporate the apples.

Spread 2 tablespoons of flour on the counter. Place the dough on the counter, and knead the dough 4 to 5 times.

Using your hands, press the dough into a 9- to 10-inch circle. Cut the dough into 8 pie slices. Place the slices on an ungreased baking sheet. Brush the tops of each scone with the milk; sprinkle the coarse sugar crystals on top of each scone.

Bake until golden brown, about 15 minutes.

TO MAKE THE FRESH CREAM TOPPING

In the bowl of a stand mixer or a large mixing bowl with a hand mixer, beat the whipping cream, sugar, and lemon juice together on low until well combined and starting to thicken so it won't splatter, about 3 minutes. Increase the speed to high and beat until thickened enough to form soft peaks, 12 to 15 minutes.

Serve the scones warm, with each scone topped with a dollop of the cream, a dab of the apple mixture, and a sprig of the fresh mint.

Store the scones in an airtight container at room temperature for 3 to 4 days. Store the whipped cream in an airtight container in the refrigerator for 1 to 2 days.

"LET THE FEAST BEGIN!"

—Albus Dumbledore

Harry Potter and the Sorcerer's Stone

DIVINATION DREAM BAR TEA TREATS

The first lesson Professor Trelawney teaches her third-year students is dream interpretation, which offers the possibility of predicting the future. Actress Emma Thompson describes her character's entrance into her classroom as "one of the oldest, cheapest gags in the book," for just as she announces that she has "the Sight," she walks into a table. She does this again, in *Harry Potter and the Prisoner of Azkaban*, when explaining the importance of dream interpretation, "for the inner eye sees sights to which the outer world is blind." As Trelawney says she sees into the future, it occurred to Thompson that she probably couldn't see anything at all in the present.

Dream bars—also known as "magic bars"—are classic seven-layer bars. These ones are made with butterscotch chips, chopped walnuts, and toasted coconut. A prediction for the future? You'll want to make these again and again.

½ cup plus 1 tablespoon butter, room temperature, divided, plus more for greasing

1 cup plus 1 tablespoon all-purpose flour, divided

1½ cups brown sugar, divided

2 eggs

½ teaspoon baking powder

¼ teaspoon salt

1 teaspoon vanilla extract

½ cup chocolate chips

½ cup butterscotch chips

1½ cups coconut

1 cup chopped walnuts

Preheat the oven to 350°F.

Grease a 9-by-13-inch cake pan with 1 tablespoon butter.

To make the base, in a large bowl, combine 1 cup flour, ½ cup brown sugar, and the remaining ½ cup butter, and mix together with a handheld pastry blender until combined well and the dough reaches a coarse consistency. Press the base dough across the bottom of the greased cake pan, and bake until slightly brown, 20 to 25 minutes.

Remove the base layer from the oven, and set aside to cool on a wire rack. Leave the oven on for when the base layer is returned to bake with the top layer.

In a large bowl, beat the eggs slightly. Add the remaining 1 cup brown sugar, remaining 1 tablespoon flour, the baking powder, salt, vanilla, chocolate chips, butterscotch chips, coconut, and walnuts. Stir until they are well combined.

Spread the topping mixture over the baked base evenly, ensuring the same amount of thickness throughout.

Bake the bars until they are browned on top and around the edges and they begin to pull away from the sides of the pan, about 15 minutes.

Let the bars cool on a wire rack. When they are cool, use a knife to cut them into 1-inch squares.

Store in an airtight container at room temperature for 3 to 4 days.

> **"IN THIS ROOM, YOU SHALL EXPLORE THE NOBLE ART OF DIVINATION."**
>
> —Sybill Trelawney
>
> *Harry Potter and the Prisoner of Azkaban*

✦ MUGGLE MAGIC ✦

Dream bars emerged in popularity in New York City and throughout the United States in the 1930s. They are a creamy, gooey, tasty confection that should be a must at teatime.

AUNT PETUNIA'S TEATIME WINDTORTE PUDDING

It is awful that the day Vernon Dursley may make the biggest deal of his career by entertaining the Masons at a dinner party, Dobby the house-elf appears, trying to prevent Harry from returning to Hogwarts. Noticing the colorful Windtorte pudding Petunia Dursley has baked for their guests, Dobby seizes the opportunity to cause trouble. Snapping his fingers, he floats the pudding from the kitchen to the living room and drops it on top of Mrs. Mason.

The cake that drifts in the direction of the Dursleys' guests was computer generated, but it was a real cake with whipped cream and sugared violets that fell onto actress Veronica Clifford's (Mrs. Mason's) head.

This Windtorte pudding is inspired by that fateful moment in *Harry Potter and the Chamber of Secrets* and served how it appears in the film, as one pudding. We do, however, recommend enjoying the cake instead of dropping it on anyone.

FOR THE MERINGUES

4 large egg whites

½ cup granulated sugar

¼ teaspoon cream of tartar

FOR THE WHIPPED CREAM

2 cups heavy whipping cream

½ cup granulated sugar

½ teaspoon fresh lemon juice

SPECIALTY TOOLS

3 Piping bags with star tips

TO MAKE THE MERINGUES

Preheat the oven to 350°F. Line three 9-by-12-inch baking sheets with parchment paper.

In the bowl of a stand mixer or with a hand mixer and a large mixing bowl, beat the egg whites, sugar, and cream of tartar until thickened and peaks form.

On one of the baking sheets, spread the meringue in a circle about the size of a 9-inch-round cake pan. Repeat with the other two baking sheets. Bake the three meringue rounds for about 50 minutes, until brown on top and firm. Remove from the oven, leave on the baking sheets, and place on the countertop to cool until they are room temperature.

TO MAKE THE WHIPPED CREAM

In the bowl of a stand mixer or with a hand mixer and a large mixing bowl, beat the whipping cream, sugar, and lemon juice together on low until well combined and starting to thicken so that it won't splatter, about 3 minutes. Increase the speed to high and beat until thickened enough to form soft peaks, 12 to 15 minutes.

CONTINUED ON PAGE 25

CONTINUED FROM PAGE 23

FOR THE BUTTERCREAM FROSTING

6 cups powdered sugar

1 cup butter, softened

2 teaspoons vanilla extract

¼ cup milk

FOR THE TOPPINGS

20 drops green food coloring

10 drops purple food coloring

15 to 20 edible or silk purple violets

30 maraschino cherries

"THEN DOBBY MUST DO IT. SIR. FOR HARRY POTTER'S OWN GOOD."

—Dobby the house-elf to Harry Potter

Harry Potter and the Chamber of Secrets

TO MAKE THE BUTTERCREAM FROSTING

In a large mixing bowl, use a hand mixer to combine the powdered sugar, butter, vanilla, and milk. Beat on high speed, until the frosting becomes thickened but is still soft enough to work with using a piping bag, about 10 minutes.

TO ASSEMBLE

Place one of the round meringues on a cake plate. Spread ⅓ of the whipped cream on top of this first layer of meringue. Place another meringue cake on top, and top with another ⅓ of the whipped cream. Place a third meringue cake on top, and top with the remaining ⅓ of the whipped cream.

Divide the frosting in half, and place each half into separate medium mixing bowls. Add 20 drops of green food coloring to one half of the frosting and 10 drops of purple food coloring to the other half. Mix the food coloring in until thoroughly combined and there are no color streaks.

Place each of the colored frostings into its own piping bag: Place the bag in a cup and roll the edges over the rim of the cup to make it easier to fill the bag. Using a star tip in each bag, pipe dollops of frosting all around the bottom layer of meringue. Pipe alternating dollops of green- and lavender-colored frosting all around the middle layer of meringue. Pipe dollops of lavender-colored frosting all around the top layer of meringue. Arrange edible or silk purple violets and maraschino cherries around the top and bottom layers of meringue.

Store in an airtight container in the refrigerator for 1 to 2 days, although it's best if eaten immediately after assembly.

HUNGARIAN HORNTAIL MINI TEA PUDDINGS

For the first task of the Triwizard Tournament in *Harry Potter and the Goblet of Fire*, the four champions must acquire a golden egg from the clutches of a dragon—Harry's is a fire-breathing Hungarian Horntail, with spikes from its head to its tail.

The dragon Harry fought in the skies above Hogwarts was digital, but the filmmakers asked for an animatronic version for Harry to encounter the night before the task. Forty feet of Hungarian Horntail was created with a head featuring movable eyes, eyelids, and nostrils. It also breathed fire: The Horntail's head was cast in fiberglass and outfitted with a fireproof snout. A flamethrower in the dragon's mouth shot a thirty-six-foot stream of dragonfire at the camera.

These miniature puddings are covered with an orange-colored buttercream frosting, then topped with homemade hard candy that evoke the flames of a dragon's fire. But don't worry—these puddings are much sweeter than any fire-breathing dragon!

FOR THE PUDDINGS

1 cup plus
   2 tablespoons butter,
   softened, divided

2 cups granulated sugar

4 eggs, room
   temperature

3 cups all-purpose flour

1 tablespoon baking
   powder

1 cup milk, room
   temperature

2 teaspoons vanilla
   extract

TO MAKE THE PUDDINGS

Preheat the oven to 350°F. Butter the cavities of a 12-cup muffin pan with 2 tablespoons butter, making sure the bottom and sides are completely covered.

In a large mixing bowl, using a handheld mixer at medium speed, beat the remaining 1 cup butter and the sugar until the mixture becomes light and fluffy, about 4 minutes.

One at a time, add the eggs to the butter and sugar mixture. After each egg is added, beat until combined well.

Place the flour and baking powder in a separate medium bowl, and use a mixing spoon to stir them together.

CONTINUED ON PAGE 28

CONTINUED FROM PAGE 27

FOR THE BUTTERCREAM FROSTING

6 cups powdered sugar

1 cup butter, softened

2 teaspoons vanilla extract

¼ cup milk

20 drops orange food coloring

FOR THE SUGAR FLAME TOPPERS

2 cups granulated sugar

⅔ cup light corn syrup

5 drops red food coloring

5 drops yellow food coloring

5 drops orange food coloring

SPECIALTY TOOLS

Pastry bag and medium round cake decorating tip

Candy thermometer

Add ¼ of the flour mixture to the butter mixture, followed by ¼ cup of milk. After each addition, beat the ingredients until they are mixed together well, about 1 minute. Repeat this three more times until all of the flour mixture and milk are mixed well. Add the vanilla, and beat to combine well, about 1 minute.

Fill each of the 12 cavities of the muffin pan ⅔ full with the batter. Be careful not to overfill the cups, or the batter will expand over the sides of the cup while baking. Place the muffin pan in the oven and bake the puddings until the edges start to brown and pull away from the pan and a knife or toothpick comes out clean when inserted in the center, 30 to 35 minutes.

Remove the puddings from the oven, and set aside to cool, about 1 hour.

TO MAKE THE BUTTERCREAM FROSTING

In a large mixing bowl, use a hand mixer to combine the powdered sugar, butter, vanilla, milk, and food coloring. Beat on high speed until the frosting becomes thickened but is still soft enough to work with using a piping bag, about 10 minutes.

TO MAKE THE SUGAR FLAME TOPPERS

In a small saucepan over high heat, combine the sugar with ¾ cup water. Stir continuously until the sugar dissolves; add the corn syrup. Stir to combine thoroughly. Bring the mixture to a boil until it reaches the hard-crack stage (300° to 310°F), 7 to 8 minutes. Use a candy thermometer to monitor the temperature of the mixture.

Separate the mixture into 3 small aluminum pans, and blend 5 drops of a food coloring into each pan: red, yellow, and orange.

Line 2 baking sheets with parchment paper. Using a separate large spoon for each color, quickly drizzle each of the sugar mixtures onto the baking sheets. Spread the sugar mixture to make pieces in a variety of widths and lengths. Use a blunt knife to trace lines in the candy flames. Add more drops of food coloring in spots to create more three-dimensional detail.

Let the sugar flames rest until they become hardened enough to stand upright on their own in the frosting of the puddings, 6 to 8 minutes.

When the puddings have cooled to room temperature, frost each one with the buttercream frosting, and top each pudding with a sugar flame topper.

Store in an airtight container at room temperature for 2 to 3 days.

✦ BEHIND THE MAGIC ✦

The Hungarian Horntail's beak was made of steel that unintentionally but happily glowed red when the fire was released.

"I'M SURE WE'RE ALL GOING TO BE VERY GOOD FRIENDS."

"THAT'S LIKELY."

—Dolores Umbridge and a sarcastic Fred and George Weasley

Harry Potter and the Order of the Phoenix

PROFESSOR UMBRIDGE'S LOAD OF WAFFLES

Professor Dolores Umbridge starts her tenure at Hogwarts by interrupting Dumbledore and making her own speech at the welcome feast in Harry's fifth year. Her words are chilling and reflect the Ministry of Magic's attempt to interfere at Hogwarts. Harry called it "a load of waffle."

The Scottish-originated idiom "a load of waffle" describes a speech that uses a lot of words but does not give any meaningful information. Although Umbridge is a bit obscure in this speech, she makes other things very clear: She doesn't like children, and she doesn't believe Harry Potter's assertion that Voldemort is back.

These mini waffles are dipped in maple syrup and sprinkled with sugar crystals so that guests can eat them with their fingers. The waffle batter is made with sour cream, to reflect Professor Umbridge's sour personality.

5 large eggs

½ cup granulated sugar

1 cup all-purpose flour

1 teaspoon salt

¼ teaspoon ground cardamom

¼ teaspoon ground cinnamon

¼ teaspoon ground ginger

1½ cups sour cream

½ stick (4 tablespoons) butter, melted, plus more butter for waffle iron

2 cups maple syrup

1 cup coarse sugar crystals

SPECIALTY TOOLS

Mini heart-shaped waffle iron

In a large mixing bowl and with a hand mixer, beat the eggs and sugar until thoroughly combined, about 3 minutes.

In a separate large mixing bowl, mix the flour, salt, cardamom, cinnamon, and ginger. Fold the egg mixture into the flour mixture, then add the sour cream. When combined thoroughly, add the melted butter.

Heat and butter the waffle iron. Pour in 1⅓ cups batter for each waffle. Follow the instructions for the waffle iron to know when the waffle is done.

Pour the maple syrup on a large plate. Place the sugar on a separate large plate. While each waffle is still warm, but cool enough to touch, dip both sides of each waffle into the syrup, followed by the sugar crystals. Serve on a platter "loaded" with waffles.

Store in an airtight container in the refrigerator for 2 to 3 days. To reheat, preheat the oven to 375°F. Place the waffles on a baking sheet in a single layer, and place them in the oven until they become crispy again around the edges and hot throughout, 20 to 25 minutes.

✦ BEHIND THE MAGIC ✦

Actress Imelda Staunton feels Umbridge believes everything she does in her work is in the right. "And what is more frightening than those people who don't question their jobs and just carry on and do it, regardless?"

PARIS PÂTISSERIE TWO-BITE LAVENDER TEATIME CANELÉS

In *Fantastic Beasts: The Crimes of Grindelwald*, Newt Scamander casts the tracking spell *Avenseguim* in Paris to locate the mysterious wizard Yusuf Kama. Newt and Jacob Kowalski wait for him at a café in the Place Cachée.

"Paris at this time was just such an extraordinary part of the world," says actor Eddie Redmayne (Newt). "It was where a melting pot of people were meeting, and new paths were being forged. This was really a time of change, a change in fashion, a change in architecture. It was an incredibly colorful and vibrant place."

Canelés, like these, surged in popularity in late 1920s Paris. It's important that copper molds are used as they're the best conductors of heat, to give these cookies a crispy shell. Beeswax and butter are the traditional ways of greasing the molds and give these treats a light, crunchy coating that seals in a moist, creamy, custardy center with a hint of lavender and rum.

3 cups milk

½ vanilla bean, split lengthwise and scraped (or ¼ teaspoon vanilla extract)

15 tablespoons butter, divided

1 cup granulated sugar

⅔ cup all-purpose flour

2 large eggs

1 large egg yolk

3 tablespoons rum

1 tablespoon chopped fresh or dried lavender buds

⅓ cup beeswax, finely chopped

In a small saucepan over high heat, combine the milk and vanilla. Bring to a boil, then remove from heat. Add 3 tablespoons butter; stir to combine. Set aside to cool.

In a large mixing bowl, use a wire whisk to whisk together the sugar and flour.

CONTINUED ON PAGE 35

CONTINUED FROM PAGE 33

SPECIALTY TOOLS

Canelé molds

Pastry brush

> "I WAS SAYING—YOU SURE
> THE GUY'S HERE THAT
> WE'RE LOOKING FOR?"
>
> "DEFINITELY. THE FEATHER
> SAYS SO."
>
> —Jacob Kowalski and Newt
> Scamander
>
> *Fantastic Beasts:*
> *The Crimes of Grindelwald*

In a separate large mixing bowl, use a wire whisk to whisk together the 2 eggs, the egg yolk, and rum. Next, whisk the egg mixture into the sugar and flour mixture; then whisk in the milk mixture. Add the lavender buds (saving a few for garnishing), and stir into the batter. Pour the batter into an airtight container and refrigerate overnight.

In a small saucepan over low heat, melt the beeswax, and add the remaining 12 tablespoons butter. Stir the wax and butter together while the mixture heats. Once it is well blended, remove from heat. Using a pastry brush, brush the insides of the canelé molds with the mixture.

Remove the batter from the refrigerator at least 1 hour before baking.

Preheat the oven to 425°F.

Pour the batter into the molds. Fill each mold only halfway, to create mini canelés.

Bake until the canelés are dark brown, about 1 hour. Remove the molds from the oven, and remove each canelé from its mold. Set them upright on a cooling rack to cool. Store in an airtight container at room temperature for 2 to 3 days.

PROFESSOR MCGONAGALL'S TRANSFIGURATIONAL STICKY TOFFEE PUDDING BITES

Professor McGonagall is head of Gryffindor house, the Transfiguration professor, and places the Sorting Hat on first-years' heads. She is also an Animagus, a witch or wizard who can change their form into that of a specific animal. McGonagall's feline form was played by a cat who already had spectacle-shaped markings around her eyes.

Crystallized ginger, apple, and citrus transform this classic British dessert into a light, bright sticky toffee pudding. Sticky pudding is sticky inside and out—inside are Medjool dates blended with brown sugar and molasses to create a gooey filling spiced with nutmeg and cardamom. And the outside is drizzled with a thick, sweet sauce made with brown sugar and Scotch whisky.

Although bite-size and tiny enough to fit on a three-tiered tea tray, these puddings should be served on individual plates because the toffee sauce can get a bit messy and transfigure other teatime bites into just-as-sticky nibbles.

FOR THE PUDDINGS

- ⅓ cup plus 1 tablespoon butter, room temperature, divided
- 1 cup Medjool dates, trimmed and pitted
- 1 teaspoon baking soda
- 1 cup boiling water
- ¼ cup diced apple
- ¼ cup crystallized ginger
- Juice of ½ medium orange
- 1 cup brown sugar
- ½ teaspoon vanilla extract
- 2 large eggs, room temperature
- 2 tablespoons molasses

TO MAKE THE PUDDINGS

Preheat the oven to 350°F. Use 1 tablespoon butter to grease the cavities of a 12-cup muffin pan. In a food processor, add the dates and baking soda, and pour the boiling water over top. Set aside to soak for about 20 minutes.

In a large bowl, mix together apples, ginger, orange juice, remaining ⅓ cup butter, brown sugar, vanilla, eggs, and molasses until thoroughly combined.

In another large bowl, mix together the flour, baking powder, salt, nutmeg, and cardamom. Combine the flour mixture with the apple mixture.

Pulse the dates, water, and baking soda until the dates become the consistency of a smooth purée; carefully fold the dates into the batter.

CONTINUED ON PAGE 38

CONTINUED FROM PAGE 37

1⅔ cups all-purpose flour

1½ teaspoons baking powder

¼ teaspoon salt

¼ teaspoon freshly grated nutmeg

¼ teaspoon cardamom

12 pointed ice-cream cones

1 tablespoon black cocoa powder (optional)

FOR THE SCOTCH WHISKY TOFFEE SAUCE

½ cup heavy whipping cream

1 stick (8 tablespoons) butter

1 cup light brown sugar

1 tablespoon Scotch whisky

1 teaspoon vanilla extract

1 pinch pink Himalayan sea salt

FOR THE FRESHLY WHIPPED CREAM TOPRING

2 cups heavy whipping cream

½ cup granulated sugar

½ teaspoon fresh lemon juice

SPECIALTY TOOLS

Witch hat–shaped edible cupcake toppers or the pointed ends of ice-cream cones

Fill each of the cavities of the prepared muffin pan ¾ full with the batter. Bake for about 20 minutes, or until a toothpick inserted into the center comes out clean.

TO MAKE THE SCOTCH WHISKY TOFFEE SAUCE

In a saucepan over high heat, combine the heavy whipping cream, butter, brown sugar, Scotch whisky, vanilla, and salt. Stir to combine well and dissolve the sugar. Bring the mixture to a boil, stirring continuously, and boil for 1 minute.

Reduce the heat to medium-low, and continue to cook until the sauce is smooth and slightly thickened, 3 to 5 minutes.

TO MAKE THE FRESHLY WHIPPED CREAM TPPPING

In the bowl of a stand mixer or a large mixing bowl and a hand mixer, beat the heavy whipping cream, sugar, and lemon juice until the cream is thickened, 12 to 15 minutes. Beat on low speed for the first 2 to 3 minutes until the cream begins to thicken.

TO ASSEMBLE EACH DESSERT

Place a pudding upside down on a dessert plate. Use a dry pastry brush to dust the sugar cone hats with the black cocoa powder and top each pudding with a cone hat or an edible witch hat cupcake decoration. Drizzle the sauce over the ice-cream-cone top and the pudding; top each dessert with a dollop of the fresh whipped cream.

Store the sauce and the puddings, separately, in airtight containers in the refrigerator for 4 to 5 days.

"THAT WAS BLOODY BRILLIANT!"

—Ron Weasley in response to Professor McGonagall's transformation from a cat

Harry Potter and the Sorcerer's Stone

MOLLY WEASLEY'S INDIVIDUAL TEATIME RHUBARB AND CUSTARD TRIFLES

Molly Weasley makes sure her family is well-fed—from eggs for breakfast to an elaborate turkey dinner for Christmas. Sharp eyes will notice a stack of cookbooks in The Burrow, including *One Minute Feasts—It's Magic!*, *Enchantment in Baking*, and *Charm Your Own Cheese*, created by the graphics department.

These creamy trifles are much like the dessert named "rhubarb fools," as they are affectionately called in England. This delicious trifle has layers of rhubarb sauce and custardy cream, a very popular English treat. Trifles are traditional at teatime, and their presentation adds to the variety of the tea, which is one of the most important aspects of entertaining during teatime.

Serve these in clear glass champagne flutes or wineglasses so that the pretty layers of roasted rhubarb, fresh cream, and shortbread crumbles are visible to your guests. For even smaller portions, they can be served in clear glass shot glasses or timbales.

FOR THE ROASTED RHUBARB

3 cups trimmed and chopped rhubarb (½-inch pieces)

¼ cup brown sugar

1 tablespoon all-purpose flour

NOTE ✦ When rhubarb is not in season, substitute 2 cups peach or marmalade preserves at room temperature.

TO MAKE THE ROASTED RHUBARB

Preheat the oven to 350°F. Line a baking sheet with parchment paper.

In a cast-iron skillet, combine the rhubarb, brown sugar, and flour, and stir until the rhubarb is thoroughly coated with the sugar-flour mixture. Place the skillet in the oven and roast until the rhubarb mixture becomes softened and easily spreadable, 15 to 20 minutes. Remove from the oven and set on the counter to cool until it is time to assemble the trifle.

CONTINUED ON PAGE 40

CONTINUED FROM PAGE 39

FOR THE SHORTBREAD BISCUITS

2 cups butter, softened

1 cup granulated sugar

4 teaspoons vanilla extract

4 cups all-purpose flour

1 teaspoon salt

2 cups ground pecans (optional)

FOR THE FRESHLY WHIPPED CREAM LAYER

2 cups heavy whipping cream

½ cup granulated sugar

½ teaspoon fresh lemon juice

FOR THE VANILLA PUDDING LAYER

3 tablespoons cornstarch

3 cups whole milk, divided

¼ teaspoon pink Himalayan sea salt

1 cup sugar

3 egg yolks

1 tablespoon butter, softened

1 vanilla bean pod, or ¼ teaspoon vanilla extract

FOR THE GARNISH

1 tablespoon chiffonade fresh mint leaves

1 tablespoon chopped fresh marjoram leaves

TO MAKE THE SHORTBREAD BISCUITS

In a large mixing bowl with a handheld mixer on medium-high speed, cream together the butter, sugar, 2 tablespoons water, and the vanilla, gradually adding in the flour and salt. Cream until fluffy and light. Add the pecans, if using, and combine well.

Fill a small ice-cream scoop with dough, and roll the dough in your hands to create 1-inch balls. Place the balls of dough 2 inches apart on the prepared baking sheet. Use the palm of your hand to press down each ball to ½-inch thickness.

Bake until the edges of the biscuits are lightly browned, 20 to 25 minutes. Remove from the oven, and set aside to cool.

TO MAKE THE WHIPPED CREAM LAYER

In a stand mixer or a large mixing bowl with a hand mixer, beat together the whipping cream, sugar, and lemon juice on low until well combined and starting to thicken so it won't splatter, about 3 minutes. Increase the speed to high and beat until thickened enough to form soft peaks, 12 to 15 minutes.

TO MAKE THE VANILLA PUDDING LAYER

In a large mixing bowl, whisk the cornstarch with ¼ cup of milk.

In a medium saucepan over medium heat, whisk together the remaining 2¾ cups milk, the salt, and sugar. Cook, stirring occasionally, until there is steam.

In a medium bowl, whisk the egg yolks. Pour ½ cup of the steamed milk into the egg yolks and stir continuously. Slowly place the egg mixture and the cornstarch mixture in the saucepan, and simmer, whisking continuously, until the mixture thickens.

Using a knife, open the vanilla bean pod, and scrape the vanilla from the pod. Discard the pod. Set the vanilla from the pod on a medium plate on the countertop.

Remove the pudding from the heat; stir in the butter and the vanilla that was scraped from the inside of the vanilla bean pod.

TO ASSEMBLE THE TRIFLES

Using your hands, crush together two shortbread biscuits at a time until all of the biscuits are coarsely crushed. Place ½ cup of the crushed biscuits into each of 6 clear wineglasses. Place ½ cup of pudding on top of the crushed biscuits. Place ½ cup of the roasted rhubarb on top of the pudding in each wineglass, followed by ½ cup of the fresh whipping cream. Top each trifle with a sprinkle of fine biscuit crumbs and fresh mint and marjoram leaves.

Store the pudding, rhubarb mixture, and whipped cream in separate airtight containers in the refrigerator for 1 to 2 days. Store the biscuits in an airtight container at room temperature for 4 to 5 days.

"YOU HUNGRY, HARRY?"

—Molly Weasley

Harry Potter and the Order of the Phoenix

✦ MUGGLE MAGIC ✦

"Fools" plays on the meaning of something described as a trifle as being inconsequential.

PROFESSOR SLUGHORN'S ONE-BITE HIGH TEA PROFITEROLES

In *Harry Potter and the Half-Blood Prince*, Potions professor Horace Slughorn hosts a dinner party for members of his newly revived "Slug Club." Dessert for the selected students is a heaping serving of mouthwatering profiteroles.

It's at this dinner that Cormac McLaggen tries to catch the attention of Hermione Granger by dipping his fingers into his bowl and cleaning them off as she watches in distress. The action was not in the script but improvised by actor Freddie Stroma as Cormac on the suggestion of director David Yates.

Profiteroles are often served in the form of a tower, but this teatime version made with a basic pâte à choux recipe offers miniature cream puffs filled with freshly whipped cream with a hint of lemon, topped with a minty chocolate sauce and garnished with a sprig of fresh chocolate mint. You won't need to lick your fingers clean like Cormac to woo your guests with these profiteroles.

FOR THE PÂTE À CHOUX

¼ cup butter, room temperature

½ cup all-purpose flour

2 eggs, room temperature

FOR THE CREAM FILLING

2 cups heavy whipping cream

½ cup granulated sugar

½ teaspoon fresh lemon juice

FOR THE MINTY CHOCOLATE SAUCE

4 ounces mint milk chocolates

¼ cup butter

1 tablespoon chiffonade fresh chocolate mint leaves

TO MAKE THE PÂTE À CHOUX

Preheat the oven to 400°F. Line a baking sheet with parchment paper.

In a large saucepan over high heat, bring ¼ cup water and the butter to a boil. When the water and butter start to boil, quickly add the flour, and stir until the mixture becomes a ball. Remove the mixture from the heat. Using a handheld mixer, beat the eggs in, one at a time, until the mixture is smooth.

Use a 1-inch ice-cream scoop to form the dough into balls, and place the balls 2½ inches apart from one another on the prepared baking sheet.

Bake until golden brown around the edges, 35 to 40 minutes. Remove them from the oven and set aside until they have cooled, about 30 minutes. Use a serrated knife to cut each of the pastries in half horizontally.

TO MAKE THE CREAM FILLING

In the bowl of a stand mixer or a large mixing bowl with a hand mixer on medium speed, beat the whipping cream, sugar, and lemon juice together on low until well combined and starting to thicken so it won't splatter, about 3 minutes. Increase the speed to high and beat the cream until thickened enough to form soft peaks, 12 to 15 minutes.

TO MAKE THE MINTY CHOCOLATE SAUCE

Melt the chocolate and butter in a double boiler over medium heat on the stovetop or in the microwave. If using the microwave, microwave in a microwave-safe bowl for 1 minute, stirring after 30 seconds.

Place the cream filling between the top and bottom pieces of each of the pastries. Drizzle 1 tablespoon of mint chocolate sauce over each profiterole, and garnish with a garnish with the mint leaves.

Store the pastry and chocolate sauce in separate airtight containers at room temperature for 1 to 2 days. Store the cream filling in an airtight container in the refrigerator for 1 to 2 days.

✦ BEHIND THE MAGIC ✦

For the most part, the food seen onscreen was faked, or a combination of both fake and real food, but as the students were actively eating the dessert, real profiteroles were served.

"... JUST IN TIME FOR DESSERT. THAT IS, IF BELBY'S LEFT YOU ANY."

—Horace Slughorn

Harry Potter and the Half-Blood Prince

KOWALSKI BAKERY'S OCCAMY EGG TEATIME SURPRISE

Jacob Kowalski is turned down for a business loan in *Fantastic Beasts and Where to Find Them*, but his friendship with Newt Scamander compels the Magizoologist to gift him a case of Occamy eggshells as collateral to start his bakery. Occamy eggshells are made of the purest silver and worth a fortune.

This teatime treat, inspired by the Occamy eggs seen in the film, is a treat within a treat! Each white chocolate Occamy egg holds another sweet surprise inside. For example, you can put in one of Professor McGonagall's Transfigurational Sticky Toffee Pudding Bites or a Two-Bite Lavender Teatime Canelé inside. To resemble the Occamy eggs in the film, they're covered with edible silver cake-decorating dust. And so guests can crack open the egg, each is served with a small wooden mallet or a tool of your choice to find the confection nestled inside.

Two 11-ounce bags white chocolate chips

2 tablespoons butter

1 tablespoon edible silver luster dust

FOR THE FILLING

Any combination of the below:

Hagrid's Pumpkin Teatime Madeleines (page 13)

One-Bite Circus Animal Tea Biscuits (page 53)

Dumbledore's Elderberry Tea Pastilles (page 143)

Disenchantment Tea Candies (page 133)

In a large microwave-safe bowl in the microwave or in a double boiler over medium heat on the stovetop, melt the white chocolate chips and butter just until the chips are melted. Use a spoon to stir until the butter and white chocolate are blended together thoroughly. If melting the chocolate in the microwave, heat the chocolate on medium for 1 minute, stir, and heat for another 1 minute.

Using a pastry brush, coat the inside of each half of the egg molds with luster dust. Pour the melted chocolate into the mold and rotate it for smooth coverage. Pull the chocolate up along the sides to the top of the egg mold all around. Repeat this multiple times all around, until the inside of each mold is covered about ¼ inch thick with chocolate. Use a clean butter knife to go around the edge of the mold, evening out chocolate around the edges.

Place the mold in the refrigerator until the chocolate sets enough to stand on its own once the mold is removed, 10 to 15 minutes.

CONTINUED ON PAGE 47

CONTINUED FROM PAGE 45

SPECIALTY TOOLS

Large silicone egg mold
4 wooden mallets for
cracking chocolate

"DEAR MR. KOWALSKI, YOU
ARE WASTED IN A CANNING
FACTORY. PLEASE TAKE
THESE OCCAMY EGGSHELLS
AS COLLATERAL FOR YOUR
BAKERY. A WELL-WISHER."

—Note from Newt
Scamander to Jacob
Kowalski

*Fantastic Beasts and Where
to Find Them*

✦ BEHIND THE MAGIC ✦

Occamys are *choranaptyxic*:
creatures that shrink or grow
according to the available
space, a word created by the
screenwriter, J.K. Rowling.

Remove the mold from the refrigerator, and pull the silicone mold away from the chocolate. Using a pastry brush, go around the edge of the top and bottom halves of the eggs with hot water so that the chocolate softens just enough so that both the top and bottom halves of the eggs will stick when they are brought together. Dust the outside of each half once more with luster dust, if desired.

Place a tiny sweet treat in the middle of one of the halves of the egg (see options from Ingredients List page 45). Bring the halves of egg together so that the edges line up, and lightly press until the halves are secured together, about 3 minutes. Place the eggs back in the refrigerator to harden together well, about 3 minutes.

Remove from the refrigerator, and let the eggs sit until room temperature, about 5 minutes.

Place the edible silver luster dust on a plate or in a shallow bowl. Roll the eggs in the dusting powder so that the powder completely covers the eggs. If enough powder does not stick, sprinkle the dust on top of the eggs when they are on a plate, ready to be served. Serve each egg with a mallet to open it.

Store the chocolate eggs in an airtight container at room temperature for 2 to 3 weeks.

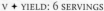
HONEYDUKES LEMON DROP MERINGUE TEATIME BITES

Within the film set for Honeydukes, seen in *Harry Potter and the Prisoner of Azkaban*, are jars and jars of Chocoballs and Exploding Bonbons, plus Licorice Wands, toffees, and Jelly Slugs (they're "wriggling good"). Tall glass dispensers of Bertie Bott's Every Flavour Beans line the mint-green walls, and there are rows of Chocolate Skeletons.

A particular favorite in the Honeydukes line of products is Sherbet Lemons, traditional British boiled sweets. *Sherbet Lemon* is used by Albus Dumbledore as the password for access to his office, which Professor McGonagall intones in *Harry Potter and the Chamber of Secrets*.

Inspired by Honeydukes' Sherbet Lemons, these teatime bites are mini deconstructed lemon meringue pies, without the crust. In the center of the meringue is a bright, lemony homemade pie filling that tastes as refreshingly tart and lemony as the lemon candies at Honeydukes.

FOR THE MERINGUES

4 large egg whites

¼ cup granulated sugar

¼ teaspoon cream of tartar

"SHERBET LEMON."

—The password to the Hogwarts headmaster's office spoken by Minerva McGonagall

Harry Potter and the Chamber of Secrets

TO MAKE THE MERINGUES

Preheat the oven to 350°F. Line a baking sheet with parchment paper.

In the bowl of a stand mixer or a large mixing bowl with a hand mixer on high speed, beat the egg whites, sugar, and cream of tartar until thickened and peaks form, 12 to 15 minutes.

Use a large ice-cream scoop to scoop 1-inch balls of the meringue, and place each ball of meringue on the prepared baking sheet about 1½ inches apart. Use a spoon to flatten each meringue to ½-inch thickness, and create a depression in the center of each of the meringues where the lemon pie filling will be placed. Bake until slightly firm, enough to hold up the lemon pudding, about 50 minutes.

CONTINUED ON PAGE 50

CONTINUED FROM PAGE 49

FOR THE LEMON PIE FILLING

1 cup granulated sugar

3 tablespoons cornstarch

3 tablespoons all-purpose flour

¼ teaspoon pink Himalayan sea salt

3 large egg yolks, beaten, room temperature

Juice and zest of 3 lemons

1 tablespoon butter

FOR THE FRESH WHIPPED CREAM

2 cups heavy whipping cream

½ cup granulated sugar

½ teaspoon fresh lemon juice

TO MAKE THE LEMON PIE FILLING

In a saucepan over high heat, combine the sugar, cornstarch, flour, 1¼ cups water, and salt. Stir continuously until the mixture bubbles lightly and thickens. Add in the egg yolks and bring the mixture to boil. Stir continuously for 2 minutes. Reduce the heat to low, and add the lemon juice, zest, and butter. Stir until blended well and there are no lumps.

TO MAKE THE FRESH WHIPPED CREAM

In the bowl of a stand mixer or a large mixing bowl with a hand mixer, beat the heavy whipping cream, sugar, and lemon juice until the cream is thickened, 12 to 15 minutes. Beat on low speed for the first 2 to 3 minutes until the cream begins to thicken, then increase to high speed for the remaining 10 to 13 minutes.

To assemble, arrange the baked meringues on a serving platter. Use a spoon to put 2 tablespoons of lemon filling in a circle in the center to top of each meringue. Spread the pie filling around in the center in a circular motion, making sure that it forms a complete circle to resemble an egg yolk. Place a dollop of fresh whipped cream on the left side of each meringue, allowing the lemon pudding to be visible.

Store in an airtight container in the refrigerator for 1 to 2 days.

✦ BEHIND THE MAGIC ✦

For filming inside the Honeydukes set, the actors were told that all the candy had been coated with a lacquer finish, but it turned out that was just a story to keep them from eating it!

ONE-BITE CIRCUS ANIMAL TEA BISCUITS

Circus animal-based cookies have been around since the dawn of the twentieth century. These whimsical tea biscuits, inspired by the magic of the Circus Arcanus where Tina Goldstein locates Credence Barebone in *Fantastic Beasts: The Crimes of Grindelwald*, are cut out in the shape of traditional Muggle circus animals and decorated in classic circus animal cookie colors, featuring white and hot pink frosting, with sprinkles of nonpareils to add pops of color, whimsy, and nostalgia to the assortment.

In addition to the exotic beasts that are showcased at Circus Arcanus, there are also some unique street vendors. The candy floss (cotton candy) stand has chin rests where the floss maker can magic a beard for patrons (a play on the French term for cotton candy, *barbe à papa*, which translates to "father's beard"). There are also candy floss–shaped balloons, with the idea being they don't have the normal gravitational issues, so the candy floss floats.

FOR THE BISCUITS

- 4 cups all-purpose flour, plus more for dusting the counter to roll out the dough
- 1 teaspoon baking soda
- 1 teaspoon baking powder
- 1 cup vegetable shortening
- 1½ cups granulated sugar
- 1½ teaspoons salt
- 1 cup sour cream
- 2 eggs, room temperature
- 1 teaspoon vanilla extract

NOTE ✦ Use cookie cutters shaped like beasts or color the cookies with frosting in unusual shades of purple or green, or mixes of both, to reflect the circus environment.

TO MAKE THE BISCUITS

Preheat the oven to 350°F. Line a baking sheet with parchment paper.

In a large bowl, combine the flour, baking soda, baking powder, shortening, sugar, salt, sour cream, eggs, and vanilla until well combined. Chill the dough in the refrigerator for about 30 minutes.

Using a rolling pin, roll out the dough onto a floured work surface.

Use miniature circus animal-shaped cookie cutters to cut out the biscuits.

Place the biscuits on the prepared baking sheet, about 1½ inches apart. Bake until lightly browned around the edges, about 10 minutes.

CONTINUED ON PAGE 55

CONTINUED FROM PAGE 53

FOR THE ICING

1 cup powdered sugar

2 tablespoons milk

4 drops red food
   coloring

½ cup multicolored
   nonpareils

SPECIALTY TOOLS

Miniature circus
   animal cookie cutters

TO MAKE THE ICING

In a large bowl, mix the powdered sugar and milk
together thoroughly until the frosting becomes a
smooth consistency.

Divide the icing in half, placing one half in a separate
bowl, and add 4 drops of red food coloring to half of the
icing.

One by one, dip half of the biscuits into the pink
frosting and the other half into the white frosting.
Quickly, before the frosting begins to dry, sprinkle each
biscuit with multicolored nonpareils.

Store at room temperature in an airtight container for
2 to 3 weeks.

"CIRQUE ARCANUS: LE PLUS GRAND DES
CIRQUES L'ÉVÉNEMENT DU SIÈCLE"

(CIRCUS ARCANUS: THE GREATEST
CIRCUS EVENT OF THE CENTURY)

—Advertising Poster for Circus Arcanus

*Fantastic Beasts: The Crimes of
Grindelwald*

QUEENIE'S MINI BRANDIED APPLE STRUDELS WITH APPLE MINT SAUCE

Queenie Goldstein uses magic to make a delicious apple strudel for Newt Scamander and Jake Kowalski when they visit the Goldstein sisters' apartment in *Fantastic Beasts and Where to Find Them*. With a delicate wave of her wand, apples are sliced, then combined with raisins and spices before being wrapped in several layers of rolled dough. Dough roses and leaves land like butterflies on the pastry, all sprinkled with a generous helping of powdered sugar.

Strudel means "whirlwind" in this national dish of Austria, recognizing the swirl of pastry and filling.

These teatime strudels are diminutive puff pastries filled with cinnamon-spiced apples cooked down with brandy and drizzled with a brandy-butter sauce. Each has a miniature braid, just like the braided strudel Queenie makes.

FOR THE STRUDELS

- 1 pound frozen puff pastry dough
- 4 large honeycrisp apples, peeled and cut into 1-inch pieces
- ½ cup raisins
- 1 cup brandy
- 2 tablespoons brown sugar
- 1 tablespoon granulated sugar
- ¼ teaspoon ground cinnamon
- ½ cup chopped walnuts
- 2 teaspoons butter
- 1 egg white

TO MAKE THE STRUDELS

Remove the pastry dough from the freezer to thaw. Line a 9-by-12-inch baking sheet with parchment paper. Preheat the oven to 375°F.

In a large bowl, marinate the apples and raisins in the brandy for 1 to 2 hours.

Strain the apples and raisins from the brandy over a large mixing bowl, and reserve the brandy to make the sauce.

In a medium saucepan over medium heat, combine the apples and raisins with the brown sugar, granulated sugar, and cinnamon. Cook until thickened, 8 to 10 minutes. Add the walnuts, and stir to incorporate. Set aside to cool.

Cut the pastry dough into eight 4-by-2-inch rectangles and 24 thin strips that are 4 inches long. Create 8 braids, one for each strudel: Using three strips side by side, cross the left strip over the center strip; then cross the right strip over the center strip, alternating, until the full length of each strip is braided.

CONTINUED ON PAGE 59

CONTINUED FROM PAGE 57

FOR THE CINNAMON-SUGAR TOPPING

¼ cup ground cinnamon

¼ cup sugar

FOR THE BRANDY-BUTTER SAUCE

1 tablespoon brown sugar

1 teaspoon butter

FOR THE GARNISH

1 cup chopped fresh apple mint

NOTE ✦ For a gluten-free option, serve this apple filling and this sauce over ½ cup of ice cream in a pretty glass dish, and garnish with a sprig of fresh apple mint.

✦ BEHIND THE MAGIC ✦

Texturing and shading were added digitally to Queenie's strudel that would mimic the appearance of the pastry cooking, and like most baked goods while they cook, the animators had it shrink down a little.

When the apple mixture is cool, place 3 tablespoons of mixture on one side of each rectangular piece of pastry dough. Leave a ½-inch border around the sides. Place ¼ teaspoon butter on top of the apple mixture on each piece of pastry dough. Fold the other side of each piece of pastry dough over the apple mixture. Use the tines of a fork to press down the dough together on the three sides where the top and bottom come together.

Place one pastry braid on one of the long sides of each strudel rectangle; press down the top of the braid in the top corner of the strudel to secure the braid. The braid will extend over the bottom edge of the pastry by ½ inch.

Lightly beat the egg white, and use a pastry brush to cover each strudel with the egg white.

Pierce the top of each strudel with a knife to create ventilation.

TO MAKE THE CINNAMON-SUGAR TOPPING

In a small bowl, combine the cinnamon and sugar.

Sprinkle the cinnamon-sugar mixture lightly on top of the strudels.

Place the strudels on the prepared baking sheet.

Bake until golden brown and flaky, 35 to 40 minutes. Remove from the oven and cool.

TO MAKE THE BRANDY-BUTTER SAUCE

In a small saucepan over medium-high heat, combine the remainder of the brandy that was used for marinating the apples and raisins with the brown sugar and butter. Bring to a boil, stirring continuously, then reduce the heat to medium-low and simmer until thickened, about 20 minutes. Remove the sauce from the heat.

Use a spoon to lightly drizzle the brandy-butter sauce over each strudel; garnish with fresh apple mint.

Store the sauce in the refrigerator in an airtight container for 5 to 6 days, and the strudels in the refrigerator in an airtight container for 3 to 4 days.

PROFESSOR SPROUT'S BITE-SIZE GREENHOUSE MYSTERY CAKES

It's possible that among the plant life Professor Sprout grows for her Herbology classes in *Harry Potter and the Chamber of Secrets* are lunch- and dinnertime staples such as tomatoes (which are a fruit!). Fortunately, tomatoes are a lot easier to work with than screaming Mandrakes or snapping Venomous Tentacula. The design of Greenhouse Three, where the second-years are taught, was inspired by a greenhouse at Kew Royal Botanic Gardens, built during the Victorian era, only a decade or so after regular afternoon teas began.

These mini puddings are a twist on the 1930s tomato soup cake with its warming nutmeg, cinnamon, and clove spiciness. The dessert was sometimes known as the mystery cake, because it would take a very discerning palate to recognize that the cake is made with a can of tomato soup! Each bite-size pudding is capped with vanilla frosting and then topped with a dollop of a sweet tomato jam.

FOR THE TOMATO SOUP PUDDINGS

1 tablespoon butter, for greasing muffin pan

3 tablespoons shortening

1 cup granulated sugar

2 eggs

One 10¾-ounce can tomato soup

2 cups all-purpose flour

1⅛ teaspoons baking soda

1 teaspoon nutmeg

1 teaspoon cloves

1 teaspoon ground cinnamon

1 cup chopped walnuts

1 cup raisins or chopped dates

FOR THE FROSTING

6 cups powdered sugar

1½ cups butter, softened

3 teaspoons vanilla extract

5 tablespoons whole milk

FOR THE TOMATO JAM

24 small multicolored mini tomatoes

2 cups granulated sugar

2 tablespoons honey

1 tablespoon vanilla extract

"WELCOME TO GREENHOUSE THREE, SECOND-YEARS. NOW GATHER 'ROUND, EVERYONE."

—Pomona Sprout

Harry Potter and the Chamber of Secrets

✦ MUGGLE MAGIC ✦

As a fun game, have your guests try to guess what the mystery ingredient is before it is revealed.

TO MAKE THE TOMATO SOUP PUDDINGS

Preheat the oven to 350°F. Grease a 12-cup muffin pan with butter.

In a large mixing bowl, using a handheld mixer on high speed, cream together the shortening and sugar. Add the eggs and beat until well combined. Add the soup and beat until well combined. In a separate large mixing bowl, use a large mixing spoon to mix the flour, baking soda, nutmeg, cloves, and cinnamon. Add the walnuts and raisins. With the same spoon, add the flour mixture to the egg mixture, and stir to combine thoroughly. Place in the prepared muffin pan.

Bake until a toothpick inserted in the middle of one of the puddings comes out clean, 35 to 40 minutes.

TO MAKE THE FROSTING

In a stand mixer or a large mixing bowl with a hand mixer on high speed, combine the powdered sugar, butter, vanilla, and milk until combined thoroughly and thickened yet spreadable, about 10 minutes.

TO MAKE THE TOMATO JAM

In a small saucepot over high heat, combine the tomatoes, 2 cups water, sugar, honey, and vanilla, and bring to a boil. Reduce the heat to medium-high, and stir occasionally until thickened, 20 to 30 minutes.

When the puddings have cooled, top each one with frosting. Serve with a dollop of tomato jam on top of each pudding.

Store the puddings at room temperature in an airtight container for 3 to 4 days. Store the tomato jam in the refrigerator in an airtight container for 4 to 5 days.

PLACE CACHÉE ORANGE-SCENTED TEATIME PASTRY PUFFS

The Place Cachée (the hidden place) is the Parisian equivalent of Diagon Alley, except this version is actually two locations in one: a shopping area for Muggles and, at the same time, the same for magical folk, entered through a bronze statue of a robed woman in a way similar to Platform 9¾. In Diagon Alley, there is a cauldron shop, and so there is a French version featuring copper jelly molds. There's also an apothecary, a wand shop, and, of course, a pâtisserie (pastry shop): *Confiserie Enchantée*.

These diminutive orange-and-almond-flavored pâte à choux pastries would be revered at any Parisian café. After being topped with a powdered sugar frosting and slivered almonds, teatime guests can eat these with their fingers in one or two bites.

FOR THE BASE CRUST LAYER

1 cup all-purpose flour

½ cup butter

FOR THE TOP LAYER

½ cup butter

1 teaspoon orange extract

1 cup all-purpose flour

3 eggs

FOR THE FROSTING

6 cups powdered sugar

1½ cups butter, softened

5 tablespoons whole milk

FOR THE TOPPING

½ cup sliced almonds

½ teaspoon freshly grated orange zest

TO MAKE THE BASE CRUST LAYER

Preheat the oven to 375°F. Line two 9-by-12-inch baking sheets with parchment paper. Use a fork or a handheld pastry blender to mix together the flour and butter. Add 2 tablespoons water, spreading it evenly across the butter and flour mixture. Mix until a dough forms. Divide the dough in half, and form two long oval shapes, thinning the dough out to about ¼ inch thick all around the oval. Place each dough oval on its own baking sheet.

TO MAKE THE TOP LAYER

In a saucepan over high heat, bring 1 cup water and the butter to a boil. Add the orange extract, remove the saucepan from the stovetop, and add the flour. Stir until it starts to pull away from the edge of the saucepan. Add the eggs in, one at a time, stirring each egg as it is added, until all 3 eggs are incorporated well.

Divide this mixture in half, and spread evenly across the top of each of the base crust layers on the baking sheets.

Bake until golden brown around the edges, about 1 hour. Remove from the oven and set aside to cool.

TO MAKE THE FROSTING

In a stand mixer or a large mixing bowl with a hand mixer, combine the powdered sugar, butter, and milk until combined thoroughly and the frosting becomes thickened yet spreadable, about 10 minutes. Beat on low speed for 1 minute to incorporate the ingredients, then increase to high speed.

When the pastries have cooled to room temperature, spread the frosting evenly across the top. Sprinkle the sliced almonds evenly across the top of each pastry before the frosting dries. Sprinkle the orange zest on top of each pastry. Cut each pastry into 1- or 2-inch-square bite-size pieces.

Store at room temperature in an airtight container for 2 to 3 days.

CONFISERIE ENCHANTÉE ~ DÉLICES SUCRÉS RAFFINÉS ~ SUBLIME BONBONS DELICATS

(ENCHANTED CONFECTIONARY–REFINED SWEET DELIGHTS–SUBLIME CANDY DELICACIES)

—Signage for the *Confiserie Enchantée* on Place Cachée in Paris

Fantastic Beasts: The Crimes of Grindelwald

✦ BEHIND THE MAGIC ✦

Although the shops on Place Cachée are never entered in *Fantastic Beasts: The Crimes of Grindelwald*, they are filled with merchandise.

HOGWARTS HOUSES FOUR-LAYER RAINBOW PETITS FOURS

Each layer of these multicolored petits fours, inspired by one of the four houses of Hogwarts, explodes with a different flavor of tea and showcases the colors of the houses the students are sorted into at Hogwarts School of Witchcraft and Wizardry.

 The red house color of Gryffindor is distinguished by raspberry or strawberry tea. Slytherin is shaded green and tastes of Moroccan mint tea. Ravenclaw blue comes from the butterfly pea flower tea leaves and blue spirulina powder, and the yellow of Hufflepuff is made with lemon-lime tea. Each petit four is topped with a very light powdered sugar glaze, then sprinkled with edible gold dust and tiny stars.

FOR THE PUDDINGS

- 1 cup plus 2 tablespoons butter, softened, divided
- 2 cups sugar
- 4 eggs, room temperature
- 3 cups all-purpose flour
- 1 tablespoon baking powder
- 1 cup milk, room temperature
- 2 teaspoons vanilla extract
- 1 tea bag raspberry or strawberry tea
- 1 tea bag Moroccan mint tea
- 1 tea bag lemon-lime tea

TO MAKE THE PUDDINGS

Preheat the oven to 350°F.

Butter four 8-inch-square cake pans with 2 tablespoons softened butter.

In a large bowl with a handheld mixer at medium speed, beat the remaining 1 cup butter and the sugar together until the mixture becomes light and fluffy, about 4 minutes.

One at a time, add the eggs to the mixture. After each egg is added, beat until combined well.

Place the flour and baking powder in a separate medium bowl, and use a spoon to stir them together.

Add ⅓ of the flour mixture to the butter mixture, followed by ⅓ of the milk; repeat this two more times until both are completely added to the butter mixture. After each addition, beat until mixed together well, about 1 minute. Add the vanilla, and beat to combine well, about 1 minute.

CONTINUED ON PAGE 66

1 tea bag butterfly pea flower tea

2 teaspoons blue spirulina powder

25 drops yellow liquid food coloring

20 drops red liquid food coloring

12 drops green liquid food coloring

FOR THE CAKE FILLING LAYER

1 cup elderberry jam

FOR THE ICING

2 cups powdered sugar

4 tablespoons milk

FOR THE GARNISH

Edible gold dust and stars

NOTE ✦ This recipe is often called a "1-2-3-4 cake," getting its name from the proportions of its base ingredients: 1 cup of butter, 2 cups of sugar, 3 cups of flour, and 4 eggs.

✦ MUGGLE MAGIC ✦

Although the numerical name is appropriate for the four houses, *petits fours* actually means "small oven." And that itself is a misnomer as these colorful pastries are not cooked in small ovens! The "small" part of the name refers to the low heat used to bake these sweet treats.

Divide the cake batter into 4 equal parts and place each part into a separate 8-inch square cake pan. Using scissors, open up each of the tea bags by cutting across the top. Mix each of the four parts batter with one of the teas and food coloring, and stir to combine well: Mix one with the raspberry or strawberry tea and the red food coloring; one with the Moroccan mint tea and the green food coloring; one with the butterfly pea flower tea and the blue spirulina powder; and one with the lemon-lime tea and the yellow food coloring.

Bake the cakes until their edges start to brown and pull away from the edges of the cake pans. The cakes are done when a knife inserted in the center of each one comes out clean, 30 to 35 minutes.

Remove from the oven, and set aside to cool in their pans, about 1 hour.

When the cakes are cool, layer them on a serving platter, placing ⅓ cup jam between each cake.

TO MAME THE ICING

In a medium bowl, combine the powdered sugar and milk until well combined and a smooth and silky frosting forms, about 7 minutes. Drizzle the icing over the top of the cake, allowing it to go over the edges of the cake.

Sprinkle the top of the cake with edible gold dust and tiny stars.

Store at room temperature in an airtight container for 2 to 3 days.

DOLORES UMBRIDGE'S I WILL MAKE SCONES

As Harry Potter serves a late afternoon detention in Dolores Umbridge's office in Harry Potter and the Order of the Phoenix, the professor drinks the traditional teatime cup of tea (filled with spoonfuls of pink sugar). Surprisingly, Umbridge does not accompany the drink with one of the most popular pastries typically served at an afternoon tea: scones. Scones are shortcake-like baked goods that are crumbly, dense, and lightly sweet.

Umbridge is far from sweet. "I think she's a monster and to be played as such," says Imelda Staunton. "I don't need to understand what she does, but from a character point of view, she believes she's doing the absolute best for that school."

Scones are the perfect confection to complement your teatime, and this recipe yields gilded, raised rounds of deliciousness. If Umbridge had accompanied her tea with something sweet, these scones would be the absolute best.

2 cups flour, plus more for the work surface

1 tablespoon baking powder

2 teaspoons sugar, plus 1 tablespoon for sprinkling

1 teaspoon salt

½ cup dried currants

¾ cup plus 2 tablespoons heavy cream

FOR THE TOPPING

1 egg white, lightly beaten with 1 teaspoon water

✦ BEHIND THE MAGIC ✦

Imelda Staunton describes Dolores Umbridge as "madness and cruelty dressed up. I'm not just a lady in a very nice array of pink outfits."

Preheat the oven to 425°F. Have ready an ungreased sheet pan.

In a large bowl, whisk together the flour, baking powder, 2 teaspoons sugar, and the salt. Using a large spoon, stir in the currants and cream just until combined. Using your hands, gently gather the dough together, kneading it against the side of the bowl until it holds together in a rough ball.

Lightly flour a work surface and turn the dough out onto it. Roll out the dough about ¾ inch thick. Using a 3-inch-round cutter, cut out rounds from the dough, pressing straight down and lifting straight up and spacing them as closely together as possible. Place the dough rounds at least 2 inches apart on the sheet pan. Gather up the dough scraps, knead briefly on the floured work surface, roll out the dough again, cut out more rounds, and add them to the pan.

Using a pastry brush, lightly brush the tops of the scones with the egg white mixture, then sprinkle evenly with the remaining sugar.

Bake the scones until golden, 10 to 12 minutes. Transfer to a wire rack to cool. Serve warm or at room temperature.

TEDDY THE NIFFLER'S TWO-BITE GOLD COIN PUDDING SANDWICHES

Even though Teddy the Niffler may be Eddie Redmayne's favorite beast in the Fantastic Beasts films, the actor describes this crafty animal as the bane of his character's existence. Nifflers are attracted to shiny objects and will go to any length to obtain them. In *Fantastic Beasts and Where to Find Them*, Teddy even squeezes into a bank security vault and stuffs his pouch with gold from the deposit boxes—something Newt cannot allow! The Magizoologist needs to relieve the Niffler of the sparkling, glittering objects he's collected.

During his research for the part, Redmayne spent time with a zoologist who worked with a baby anteater. "It would curl up into a little ball, and in order to make it relax, she would tickle his little belly," says Redmayne. So, in order to make Teddy release the gold and other glittering objects he has acquired, Newt tickles him.

Every Niffler would be attracted to these lemon-flavored whoopie cakes chockful with a buttery filling and sprayed with edible gold luster dust.

FOR THE SANDWICH PUDDINGS

2 cups all-purpose flour

1¼ teaspoons baking soda

¼ teaspoon salt

1 cup granulated sugar

½ cup butter

1½ teaspoons vanilla extract

1 large egg, room temperature

Juice and zest from 1 lemon

1 teaspoon yellow food coloring

¾ cup whole milk

FOR THE FILLING

6 cups powdered sugar

1½ cups butter, softened

3 teaspoons vanilla extract

5 tablespoons whole milk

1 tablespoon edible gold sprinkles

FOR THE GARNISH

½ cup edible gold luster dust and star-shaped nonpareils

> "FOR THE LAST TIME. YOU PILFERINGGPEST–PAWS OFF WHAT DOESN'T BELONG TO YOU!"
>
> —Newt Scamander
> *Fantastic Beasts and Where to Find Them*

TO MAKE THE SANDWICH PUDDINGS

Preheat the oven to 350°F. Line a baking sheet with parchment paper.

In a large bowl, combine the flour, baking soda, and salt until well blended. Set aside.

In the bowl of a stand mixer or a large bowl with a hand mixer on high speed, cream together the sugar and butter until light, fluffy, and well blended. Mix in the vanilla, egg, lemon juice and zest (reserving ⅓ of the zest to sprinkle on top), and the food coloring; combine well.

Beat in half of the flour mixture, followed by half of the milk; and then repeat until everything is incorporated and blended well.

Use an ice-cream scoop to create balls with the dough. Place the balls of dough 2 inches apart on the prepared baking sheet. Bake until firm and a little bit browned around the edges, 10 to 15 minutes. Remove from the oven, and set aside to cool.

TO MAKE THE FILLING

In the bowl of a stand mixer or a large mixing bowl with a hand mixer, combine the powdered sugar, butter, vanilla, and milk. Mix on medium speed until combined thoroughly and the frosting becomes thickened yet spreadable, about 10 minutes.

When the puddings have cooled, assemble the sandwiches: Spread frosting on the bottom pudding, and place another pudding on top of the frosting. Spread the edible gold sprinkles on a plate. Before the frosting dries, roll each of the pudding sandwiches in the plate of sprinkles so that sprinkles are all around each of the sandwiches. Sprinkle some of the edible gold luster dust and star-shaped nonpareils on top of each sandwich; sprinkle the remaining ⅓ of lemon zest on top for extra flavor and decoration.

Store at room temperature in an airtight container for 2 to 3 days.

"HEY, KNOCK IT OFF."

—Queenie Goldstein to a hovering teapot
who won't stop nudging her for more tea

Fantastic Beasts: The Crimes of Grindelwald

QUEENIE GOLDSTEIN'S FLOATING TEAPOT

Queenie Goldstein finds herself alone and lost in Paris, unable to find her sister, Tina, in *Fantastic Beasts: The Crimes of Grindelwald*. She is "befriended" by Vinda Rosier, an acolyte of Gellert Grindelwald. At their chateau, Vinda tries to persuade Queenie to join their cause and offers her tea from a floating teapot. Queenie is not convinced and wants to leave, but the teapot keeps hovering in midair, nudging her, intent on refilling her cup.

This dish takes teatime to a new level, with its own floating teapot, creating an enchanting centerpiece for presenting sweeteners for your tea, including honey, bright pink sugar hearts, and candied ginger. There are also other tea condiments: lemon, cream, and mint. To cut little sprigs of fresh mint for the tea, a pair of manicure scissors hangs on a ribbon from the teapot! If your teapot isn't ready in (tea) time, you can circle the sweeteners and condiments around a non-floating teapot.

FOR THE CANDIED GINGER

1 cup fresh ginger, peeled and chopped into ½-inch pieces

2 cups granulated sugar, divided

FOR THE SUGAR HEARTS

1 cup bright pink sugar crystals

SPECIALTY TOOLS

1-inch heart-shaped silicone mold

TO MAKE THE CANDIED GINGER

Place the ginger, 2 cups water, and 1 cup sugar in a saucepan over high heat, and bring to a boil. Reduce the heat to medium and simmer for 1 hour.

Remove the ginger, and strain it. Discard the sugar water. In a small mixing bowl, toss the ginger in the remaining 1 cup sugar. Set aside to dry and cool, about 30 minutes. Pull the ginger pieces from the sugar, and place them in a serving dish.

TO MAKE THE SUGAR HEARTS

In a medium mixing bowl, combine the pink sugar and 1 teaspoon water until all of the sugar is somewhat moistened and reaches a tacky consistency, about 1 minute. Pack 2 or 3 pinches of the mixture into a 1-inch heart-shaped silicone mold. Pack the sugar in evenly and firmly, ensuring there are no open pockets in the mold.

Cover a countertop with a sheet of waxed paper. Push the sugar hearts out of the molds and onto the waxed paper. Let the hearts rest to become firm, about 30 minutes. For best results, cover the hearts with another sheet of waxed paper, and let sit for 4 to 6 hours or overnight. Place them in a small serving bowl.

CONTINUED ON PAGE 72

CONTINUED FROM PAGE 71

FOR THE FLOATING TEAPOT CENTERPIECE

One 18-ounce bottle of a very strong waterproof polyurethane adhesive

1 tea tray

1 teacup and saucer

One 12-inch metal barspoon

1 small teapot, preferably a silver pot with an attached lid

1 large bunch fresh mint

One 12-inch, thin ribbon

1 pair of manicure scissors

1 large lemon, cut into thin slices, quartered

1 cup cream

2 cups honey

5 clear glass bowls or teacups

1 set of sugar cube tongs

NOTE ✦ If you do not have a mold, use your fingers to roll the sugar into tiny balls.

TO MAKE THE FLOATING TEAPOT CENTERPIECE

Apply 2 tablespoons of the polyurethane adhesive on the tea tray where the tea saucer will be placed. Set the saucer on top of the adhesive. Apply 1 tablespoon of the polyurethane adhesive to the top of the saucer, and set the teacup on top of the polyurethane adhesive. Let this sit until the polyurethane adhesive hardens, about 4 hours. Place a heavy object on top to help secure the items as they set and the adhesive dries.

Bend the barspoon up on an angle at the bottom, and down on an angle at the top, so that the spoon is curved on both ends in a shape that will fit along the side of the inside of the teacup and into the spout of the teapot.

Fill the teacup ⅓ full with the polyurethane adhesive, and place the round end of the spoon in the polyurethane adhesive. Place something alongside the spoon to support it while the polyurethane adhesive hardens. Let this sit until it hardens, at least 4 hours, but preferably overnight.

When the polyurethane adhesive has hardened, and the barspoon is secure, lay the tea tray on its side, using towels to prop up spots that don't reach the table, and put the top of the barspoon into the spout of the teapot. Generously apply the polyurethane adhesive to secure the top of the barspoon inside the spout of the teapot. Let the adhesive harden for at least 24, but up to 48, hours.

When it is time to serve, cover the spots where there is hardened polyurethane adhesive with plastic wrap. Fill the teapot and teacup with fresh mint, and wrap fresh mint around the barspoon so that it is no longer visible. Be sure that the mint does not come in contact with the hardened polyurethane adhesive. Use the ribbon to tie the manicure scissors to the teapot for guests to use to clip bits of fresh mint for their tea.

Place the lemon, cream, honey, candied ginger, and sugar hearts each in separate clear glass bowls. Set the sugar cube tongs in the dish with the sugar hearts.

Store the cream, candied ginger, lemon, and fresh mint in the refrigerator in separate airtight containers for 1 to 2 days. Store the sugar hearts at room temperature in an airtight container for 3 to 4 weeks.

CHAPTER TWO

SAVORY TEATIME FINGER FOODS

DURMSTRANG INSTITUTE SHOPSKA SALAD TEA PARTY BOATS

Shopska salad is the Bulgarian national salad, and its ingredients evoke the colors of the Bulgarian flag with rich, red diced tomatoes; green cucumbers and parsley; and white onions and *tvorog* (farmer cheese). The classic Eastern European salad here is served in bite-size endive leaves that evoke Durmstrang's ship.

For his part as Durmstrang champion, Stanislav Ianevski (Durmstrang champion Viktor Krum) learned how to scuba dive for the second task of the Triwizard Tournament, which takes place under the Black Lake. He also learned how to dive from a platform for a scene where Viktor jumps off the Durmstrang ship, but unfortunately the scene did not make it to the final cut of the film.

FOR THE SHOPSKA SALAD

- 6 large vine-ripened tomatoes, diced
- 2 large English cucumbers, skin on; sliced into tiny wedges
- 1 large poblano pepper, trimmed, seeded, and diced
- 1 large bunch parsley, chopped stems removed
- ½ cup diced red onion
- 2 cups feta cheese

TO MAKE THE SHOPSKA SALAD

In a large mixing bowl, combine the tomatoes, cucumbers, poblano, parsley, onion, and feta cheese. Set aside.

TO MAKE THE DRESSING

Use a grater to zest the oranges into a large mixing bowl and set aside. Cut the oranges in half, and squeeze the juice of the oranges into a salad dressing shaker; add the honey, champagne vinegar, olive oil, garlic, salt, and peppercorns, and shake until combined well and the consistency of the dressing becomes milky. In place of a salad shaker, use a large mixing spoon to stir the ingredients together in a large mixing bowl.

Pour the dressing over the salad, and mix until the dressing thoroughly coats the salad.

CONTINUED ON PAGE 78

CONTINUED FROM PAGE 77

FOR THE DRESSING

2 medium oranges

¼ cup honey

1 tablespoon
champagne vinegar

2 tablespoons extra-
virgin olive oil

2 garlic cloves, minced

1 pinch pink
Himalayan sea salt

1 pinch freshly ground
multicolored
peppercorns

FOR PRESENTING THE SALAD

1 head radicchio
lettuce

4 heads Belgian endive

NOTE ✦ If you cannot find
an imported Bulgarian
tvorog cheese, also known
as white brine *sirene*, any
Greek or American feta
cheese will do.

Cover a serving platter one-layer-deep with radicchio leaves; arrange the endive leaves on top. Try to use the endive leaves that are in the best condition. Fill each leaf with the salad, making sure that each of the ingredients are in each of the leaves.

Garnish with the orange zest.

Store in the refrigerator in an airtight container for 1 to 2 days.

> "AND NOW OUR FRIENDS FROM THE NORTH—
> PLEASE GREET THE PROUD SONS OF DURMSTRANG."
>
> —Albus Dumbledore
>
> *Harry Potter and the Goblet of Fire*

MINI FRIED RAVEN EGG TEA SANDWICHES

During his time at Hogwarts, seen in *Fantastic Beasts: The Crimes of Grindelwald*, shy, focused Hufflepuff Newt Scamander befriends the troubled, aristocratic Slytherin Leta Lestrange. Looking for a place to hide after a particularly bad incident, Leta stumbles upon a tower sanctuary where Newt tends to helpless beasts—including a newly hatched raven chick.

"It's their oddness that brings them together," says Zoë Kravitz (Leta). "Newt is such a compassionate person. He loves the things that no one else will love, and Leta is that in a lot of ways. He sees this sad beast, or as Leta would say, a monster, in her and loves that about her, doesn't want to change a thing about her."

These two-bite tea sandwiches are made with eggs—chicken, not raven!—fried "over easy" and sprinkled with cheddar cheese and pepper. They're served on quarters of toasted bread, and then sprinkled with a hot Hungarian paprika inspired by Leta's tempestuous nature.

6 large slices wheat rye bread

2 tablespoons butter

12 large eggs

¼ teaspoon salt

¼ teaspoon freshly ground peppercorns

2 tablespoons grated cheddar cheese

1 pinch hot Hungarian paprika

NOTE ✦ For a gluten-free savory teatime treat, serve the fried eggs without the bread or with your favorite gluten-free bread.

Toast the bread, and cut the crusts from around the edges of each slice. Cut each slice into quarters.

In a frying pan over medium heat, melt the butter.

Fry the eggs until the yolks are solid but still soft, about 2 minutes on each side. Sprinkle the eggs with the salt, pepper, and cheese.

Use a spatula to separate the eggs so that there are 12 cooked eggs, each with a yolk.

Place an egg on top of each of the toast quarters, removing the white edges or flipping them over on top, to make each egg fit on the toast quarter. Top each egg with another quarter. Secure each sandwich with a bamboo pick.

Arrange the sandwiches on a platter to serve; sprinkle the tops of the sandwiches with the hot Hungarian paprika.

Store the eggs in the refrigerator in an airtight container for 2 to 3 days. Store the bread at room temperature in an airtight container for 3 to 4 days.

SALADE NIÇOISE TEATIME BOAT BITES

After they debark the Hogwarts Express, first-year students are ferried across the Black Lake before arriving at the Great Hall. Alfred Enoch, who plays Gryffindor Dean Thomas, says he will never forget the experience of crossing the lake in the small, lantern-lit boats. The filmmakers had built a shallow, but vast, tank in the studio, with metal pulleys that "sailed" the boats. "When I saw it in the cinema, it seemed so effortless," he remembers. "That was one of the first times I saw what was behind the magic, as it were. Although it gives an appearance of absolute smoothness, putting these things together isn't effortless, and I appreciated the hard work and craftsmanship that happens behind it."

Inspired by these boats in *Harry Potter and the Sorcerer's Stone*, these individual two-bite servings of radicchio leaves are filled with lemony baked tuna, roasted potatoes, green beans, hard-boiled egg, tomato, and salty kalamata olives, bathed in a light, tangy Dijon mustard dressing that will really float your boat!

FOR THE TUNA

3 tablespoons butter, softened, divided

Two 8-ounce tuna steaks

1 lemon

¼ teaspoon salt

¼ teaspoon freshly ground peppercorns

½ cup fresh chopped dill, divided

FOR THE ROASTED BABY POTATOES

1 tablespoon butter

1 cup chopped baby potatoes (½-inch square pieces)

1 garlic clove, minced

¼ teaspoon pink Himalayan sea salt

¼ teaspoon freshly ground multicolor peppercorns

FOR THE SALAD

3 large eggs, hard-boiled and chopped into ½-inch-square pieces

2 medium vine-ripened tomatoes, chopped into ½-inch-square pieces

½ cup chopped green beans (½-inch pieces)

¼ cup pitted and chopped kalamata olives (½-inch pieces)

1 head radicchio lettuce

FOR THE SALAD DRESSING

½ cup Dijon mustard

2 tablespoons champagne vinegar

Juice of 1 lemon

1 garlic clove, minced

¼ teaspoon salt

¼ teaspoon freshly ground black pepper

¼ teaspoon sugar

TO MAKE THE TUNA

Preheat the oven to 375°F. Use 1 tablespoon butter to grease the inside of a pie plate or an 8-by-8-inch-square baking dish.

Rinse the tuna steaks, and put them in the dish. Cut the lemon in half, and cut one half of the lemon into thin slices. Squeeze the other lemon half over the tuna, and place a half of a thin slice of lemon on top of each tuna steak. Place 1 tablespoon butter on top of each tuna steak; sprinkle each tuna steak with the salt and pepper and ¼ cup of the dill.

Bake the tuna until it flakes easily with a fork, about 30 minutes. The internal temperature should be 125°F.

Set the tuna aside for a few minutes to cool; then place in the refrigerator.

Leave the oven on at 375°F to roast the potatoes.

TO MAKE THE ROASTED BABY POTATOES

Use the butter to grease a pie plate or an 8-inch-square baking dish, and place the potatoes in the dish. Toss the potatoes with the garlic and sprinkle with salt and pepper.

Roast the potatoes in the oven until golden brown and a little crispy around the edges, 10 to 12 minutes, stirring after 8 minutes. Set aside to cool to room temperature.

Flake the tuna steaks to make ½-inch pieces.

TO MAKE THE SALAD

In a large bowl, combine the potatoes, eggs, tomatoes, beans, and olives.

TO MAKE THE SALAD DRESSING

In a salad dressing shaker, combine the mustard, champagne vinegar, lemon juice, garlic, salt, pepper, and sugar, and shake until blended together thoroughly, about 20 revolutions. In place of a salad shaker, use a large mixing spoon to stir the ingredients together for 30 revolutions in a large mixing bowl.

Add the dressing to the salad, and gently stir to ensure that the dressing coats all of the ingredients well. Add the tuna, and lightly fold in, turning only 2 to 3 times so that the tuna does not shred.

Pick out 16 of the sturdiest, smallest radicchio leaves. Fill each of the leaves with the salad, ensuring that each of the ingredients is in each of the leaves. Arrange the leaves on a platter, sprinkle the remaining ¼ cup fresh chopped dill on top, and serve.

Store in the refrigerator in an airtight container for 2 to 3 days.

"RIGHT THEN! FIRST-YEARS! THIS WAY, PLEASE!"

—Rubeus Hagrid

Harry Potter and the Sorcerer's Stone

RON WEASLEY'S FINGER SANDWICH BITES

When the trolley witch comes around on the Hogwarts Express with a cart filled with confections, Ron Weasley doesn't take her up on the offer—he's brought a sandwich from home, though he doesn't seem enthusiastic about it.

For the scene in the train carriage, where Harry and Ron first meet, "we were sitting opposite each other, and we were constantly giggling," says Rupert Grint (Ron). "We couldn't film it together, in fact, so we had to do it separately. [Director] Chris Columbus would play Harry's part when they were filming me, and then he would play me with Dan."

This tasty dish is inspired by sandwiches Ron probably wished he'd had on the train: Tomato and Bacon, Egg Salad, and Deviled Ham. Arrange this variety of sandwiches on a platter, and garnish with cornichons, pickle slices, or olives on sprigs of rosemary poked into the tops of a few of the sammies.

TOMATO AND BACON SANDWICHES

8 ounces bacon

2 vine-ripened tomatoes

1 teaspoon granulated sugar

4 slices caraway bread

1 cup mayonnaise

¼ cup chiffonade fresh tarragon

1 teaspoon fresh lemon juice

¼ teaspoon pink Himalayan sea salt

¼ teaspoon freshly ground black pepper

¼ teaspoon hot Hungarian paprika

FOR GARNISH

Fresh thyme leaves

TO MAKE THE SANDWICHES

Preheat the oven to 350°F. Spread the bacon strips out flat on a baking sheet, and bake until crispy, about 30 minutes.

Remove the bacon from the oven, and set it on a plate lined with paper towels until it cools to room temperature.

Slice the tomatoes into ¼-inch-thick slices; sprinkle with the sugar.

TO MAKE THE SANDWICH SPREAD

In a food processor, combine the mayonnaise, tarragon, lemon juice, salt, pepper, and paprika. Pulse everything together 3 times. Use a spoon to scrape the mixture from the sides of the food processor and pulse 2 or 3 more times until combined thoroughly.

Use a knife to remove the crusts from the bread slices. Smear some of the sandwich spread on a piece of bread. Place a thin slice of tomato on top, and place 3 strips of crispy bacon on top of the tomato. Place a second piece of bread on top. Repeat to make a second sandwich. Cut the sandwiches down the middle both ways, creating quarters. Sprinkle fresh thyme leaves on top of the sandwiches.

CONTINUED ON PAGE 84

CONTINUED FROM PAGE 83

EGG SALAD SANDWICHES

4 eggs, hard-boiled

1 cup mayonnaise

¼ cup mustard

¼ teaspoon pink Himalayan sea salt

¼ teaspoon freshly ground peppercorns

4 slices marble rye bread

1 tablespoon fresh thyme leaves

DEVILED HAM SANDWICHES

8 ounces ground ham

½ cup mayonnaise

2 tablespoons sweet pickle relish

1 tablespoon chopped celery

½ tablespoon diced red onion

¼ teaspoon freshly ground peppercorns

4 slices white bread

6 to 8 cornichons

6 to 8 sprigs fresh rosemary

TO MAKE EGG SALAD SANDWICHES

In a mixing bowl, use a masher to mash the eggs. Add the mayonnaise, mustard, salt, and pepper, and mix to combine well.

Use a knife to remove the crusts from the bread slices, and cut each slice in half horizontally. Place the egg salad between the pieces of bread. Cut the sandwiches down the middle both ways, creating quarters. Sprinkle fresh thyme leaves on top of the sandwiches.

TO MAKE DEVILED HAM SANDWICHES

In a mixing bowl, combine the ham, mayonnaise, pickle relish, celery, onion, and peppercorns.

Use a knife to remove the crusts from the bread slices, and cut each slice in half. Place the ham salad between the pieces of bread. Cut the sandwiches down the middle both ways, creating quarters. Top each sandwich with a cornichon on a sprig of rosemary.

Store the sandwich fillings in the refrigerator in separate airtight containers for 2 to 3 days. Store the breads at room temperature in airtight containers for 4 to 5 days.

"ANYTHING OFF THE TROLLEY, DEARS?"

"NO, THANKS. I'M ALL SET."

—Trolley Witch and Ron Weasley
Harry Potter and the Sorcerer's Stone

LEAKY CAULDRON
SPLIT PEA TEATIME SOUP

Harry Potter is first taken to the wizarding world's most popular pub and inn, the Leaky Cauldron, by Hagrid in *Harry Potter and the Sorcerer's Stone*, where he learns he is The Boy Who Lived. In *Harry Potter and the Prisoner of Azkaban*, after storming out of Privet Drive, he takes the Knight Bus to the Leaky Cauldron, where he meets with Minister for Magic Cornelius Fudge. Fudge offers him pea soup, which Harry declines—he's been warned about it by Dre Head, the shrunken head on the bus.

In developing a menu for the Leaky Cauldron for *Sorcerer's Stone*, the graphics department included a cauldron full of potential soup entrées, posted on a sign in the tavern, including Leaky House Soup; House Soup Leaky; Leaky, Leaky Soup; and Soup, Soup, Soup.

This soup won't eat you and is in fact a classic split pea soup made with split peas, carrots, celery, onions, and ham. Serve it warm, in individual teacups, clear coupe glasses, or ceramic ramekins.

One 16-ounce bag dried green split peas

1 ham bone with plenty of meat on it

1 medium or large red or yellow onion, chopped

1 teaspoon salt

½ teaspoon pepper

4 bay leaves

1 small bag carrots (about 10 sticks), chopped into dime-size pieces

5 sticks celery, chopped into dime-size pieces

Using a strainer, rinse the peas in cold water and let drain for a few minutes. In a large pot or Dutch oven over high heat, cover the peas with 2 inches of water. Boil for 3 minutes, and then take off heat and let soak for up to 8 hours (or overnight). Using a strainer, rinse the peas and then drain.

In a large pot or Dutch oven over high heat, place the peas, 9 cups water, the ham bone, onion, salt, pepper, and bay leaves. Bring to a boil and then reduce the heat to medium and simmer for 90 minutes, stirring occasionally.

Take out the ham bone and trim the meat; dice the meat and put the diced meat back into the pot. Add the carrots and celery. Continue to simmer for about 1 hour or until the peas and water are no longer separate. Stir throughout.

Serve in clear coupe glasses or, for a smaller option, in clear glass shot glasses.

Store in the refrigerator in an airtight container for 3 to 4 days.

> "IF YOU HAVE PEA SOUP, MAKE SURE YOU EAT IT BEFORE IT EATS YOU."
>
> —Dre Head to Harry Potter
>
> *Harry Potter and the Prisoner of Azkaban*

FORBIDDEN FOREST MINI MUSHROOM STRUDELS

The Forbidden Forest appeared in each Harry Potter film with the exception of *Harry Potter and the Deathly Hallows – Part 1* (though Harry, Ron, and Hermione spend time in several other forests). The massive, mist-filled Forbidden Forest became more theatrical and more frightening each time it was entered. For *Harry Potter and the Order of the Phoenix*, production designer Stuart Craig redesigned the trees' roots after tropical mangrove trees, which looked to him as though the trunks were supported by fingers.

These bite-size savory strudels, stuffed with mushrooms that have been sautéed in white wine, red onion, thyme, and garlic, offer a very earthy dish inspired by the plant life that would be prevalent along the base of the trees in the mysterious forest.

1 pound frozen puff pastry dough

4 tablespoons butter, softened, divided

4 cups sliced mushrooms

½ cup dry white wine

1 tablespoon plus 1 teaspoon fresh thyme leaves

1 tablespoon diced red onion

1 garlic clove, minced

1 egg white

✦ BEHIND THE MAGIC ✦

The biggest forest was built for *Harry Potter and the Deathly Hallows – Part 2*, where a cyclorama backdrop circling the set was six hundred feet in length.

Preheat the oven to 350°F. Line a 9-by-12-inch baking sheet with parchment paper.

Remove the pastry dough from the freezer to thaw.

In a large skillet over high heat, melt 2 tablespoons butter. Add the mushrooms, wine, 1 tablespoon thyme, onion, and garlic. Bring to a bubble, and then reduce the heat to medium and simmer until the wine is cooked out, 20 to 25 minutes.

Remove from the heat, and set aside to cool.

Cut the pastry dough into eight 4-by-2-inch rectangles and twenty-four ¼-inch-thick strips that are 4 inches long. Create 8 braids, one for each strudel: Using three strips side by side, cross the left strip over the center strip; then cross the right strip over the center strip, alternating, until the full length of each strip is braided.

CONTINUED ON PAGE 88

CONTINUED FROM PAGE 87

When the mushroom mixture is cool, place 3 tablespoons of mixture on one side of each rectangular piece of pastry dough. Leave a ½-inch border around the sides. Place ¼ teaspoon butter on top of the mushroom mixture on each piece of pastry dough. Fold the other side of each piece of pastry dough over the mushroom mixture. Use the tines of a fork to press down the dough together on the three sides where the top and bottom come together.

Place one pastry braid on one of the long sides of each of the strudels; press down the top of the braid in the top corner of the strudel to secure the braid. The braid will extend over the bottom edge of the pastry by ½ inch.

Lightly beat the egg white, and use a pastry brush to cover each strudel with the egg white.

Pierce the top of each strudel with a knife to create ventilation. Place the strudels on the prepared baking sheet. Bake until golden brown and flaky, 35 to 40 minutes.

Garnish with the remaining 1 teaspoon fresh thyme.

Store in the refrigerator in an airtight container for 2 to 3 days.

GF, V ✦ YIELD: 4 SERVINGS

LUNA LOVEGOOD'S HONEY-ROASTED RADISH SALAD

Growing outside the Lovegood house are orange-colored floating Dirigible Plum bushes that must have compelled daughter Luna into creating a pair of earrings based on the fruit, as seen in *Harry Potter and the Order of the Phoenix*. However, when costume designer Jany Temime first assigned the earrings to a crafter to construct, they arrived in the shape of red radishes. Actress Evanna Lynch (Luna), a well-informed Harry Potter fan, advised Temime that the earrings needed to be refashioned to match the fruit—in fact, Lynch crafted her proper earrings herself, seen onscreen.

This warm teatime salad of colorful Easter egg radishes and herbs gives a great dose of potassium and vitamin C in this pretty and flavorful side salad. The dish can be served either as a salad to pass around, or individually to each guest in a clear glass dish, wineglass, or champagne flute, to show the pretty colors of the radishes.

FOR THE ROASTED RADISHES

3 bunches fresh Easter egg radishes

2 garlic cloves, minced

1 tablespoon honey

FOR THE DRESSING

1 tablespoon champagne vinegar

½ tablespoon extra-virgin olive oil

¼ teaspoon freshly ground black pepper

1 pinch salt

1 pinch granulated sugar

"KEEP OFF THE DIRIGIBLE PLUMS"

—Sign outside the Lovegood house

Harry Potter and the Deathly Hallows – Part 1

TO MAKE THE ROASTED RADISHES

Preheat the oven to 350°F. Line a baking sheet with parchment paper.

Clean and trim the radishes; cut the large radishes in half. Chiffonade some of the radish leaves.

In a large mixing bowl, lightly toss the radishes with the garlic and honey.

Arrange the radishes and some of the leaves (reserve 2 leaves, chiffonade, for garnish) on the prepared baking sheet. Bake until the edges of the radishes start to turn light brown, 15 to 20 minutes.

Remove from the oven and set aside to cool.

TO MAKE THE DRESSING

Combine the champagne vinegar, olive oil, pepper, salt, and sugar in a salad shaker, and shake for 20 revolutions. In place of a salad shaker, use a large mixing spoon to stir the ingredients well in a large mixing bowl.

When the radishes have cooled, pour the dressing over them in a large mixing bowl, and lightly toss them. Arrange the radish salad on a plate. Lightly scatter some of the chiffonade fresh radish leaves on top for color.

Store in the refrigerator in an airtight container for 3 to 4 days, but it's best if eaten immediately while fresh and warm.

BLACK LAKE COD CAKES WITH POACHED EGGS AND BRANDY CREAM SAUCE

During the second task of the Triwizard Tournament in *Harry Potter and the Goblet of Fire*, Harry encounters the merpeople that live in the waters of the Black Lake. These underwater creatures are far from what Muggles call a mermaid. They are, as creature designer Nick Dudman describes them, nothing to tangle with.

The merpeople animators melded the creature's fish and human characteristics instead of presenting them as a human with a fish tail. Basing the design on a sturgeon, they added sea anemone–like hair, and a scythe-like fish tail that moves side to side, like a typical fish, instead of up and down.

These cod cakes offer another engaging combination by covering each with a soft poached egg topped with a brandy cream sauce flavored with paprika, multicolored peppercorns, and red pepper flakes. Serve these on small plates arranged on a table or a side buffet.

FOR THE COD CAKES

- 3 teaspoons butter, divided
- 2 fillets cod or other whitefish (about 1 pound)
- Juice from 1 lemon
- ¼ teaspoon salt
- ¼ teaspoon freshly ground black pepper
- 1 cup crushed crackers
- 1 cup chopped fresh parsley, divided
- 2 large eggs
- 2 tablespoons finely chopped red onion
- 1 small garlic clove, minced
- 1 teaspoon dry ground mustard
- ¼ cup whole milk

FOR THE BRANDY CREAM SAUCE

- 2 cups heavy whipping cream
- 2 tablespoons brandy
- ¼ teaspoon crushed red pepper flakes
- 1 pinch pink Himalayan sea salt
- 1 pinch freshly ground multicolored peppercorns
- 4 tablespoons paprika, divided

FOR THE POACHED EGGS

- 1 teaspoon vinegar
- 4 large eggs

FOR THE GARNISH

- 1 large lemon, cut into ½-inch wedges

> "MYRTLE... THERE AREN'T MEEPEOPLE IN THE BLACK LAKE. ARE THERE?"
>
> —Harry Potter to Moaning Myrtle
>
> *Harry Potter and the Goblet of Fire*

TO MAKE THE COD CAKES

Preheat the oven to 350°F. Use 1 teaspoon butter to grease an 8-inch-square baking dish or a pie plate.

Rinse the fish fillets in cold water. Place the fish fillets in the prepared baking dish. Squeeze the juice of half of the lemon over the fish; sprinkle salt and pepper on top, and lay 1 teaspoon butter on top of each filet.

Bake the fish until lightly browned around the edges and starting to pull away from the baking dish around the edges, 30 to 40 minutes. Remove from the oven, and set aside until cool enough to work with to form the fish cakes, about 5 minutes. Leave the oven on.

Using a fork, flake the fish. In a large mixing bowl, use your hands to combine the fish with the crushed crackers, ¾ cup parsley, the eggs, the other half of the lemon juice, onion, garlic, ground mustard, and milk until the mixture becomes a consistency that can be formed into 4 round fish cakes. Each fish cake should be about 3 inches round and ½ inch high.

In a separate large baking dish, bake the fish cakes until the edges are golden brown and start to pull away from the baking dish, 30 to 40 minutes. Remove them from the oven and set aside until assembly.

TO MAKE THE BRANDY CREAM SAUCE

In a medium saucepan over high heat, bring the cream to a boil. Reduce the heat to medium-high, and stir occasionally as it continues to cook and thicken, about 10 minutes. Add the brandy, red pepper flakes, salt, pepper, and 3½ tablespoons paprika. Stir well to combine. Continue cooking until the sauce thickens, 25 to 30 minutes.

TO MAKE THE POACHED EGGS

Fill a large saucepan with 6 cups water over high heat. Bring the water to a boil and then reduce the heat to medium. As the water simmers, add the vinegar, and stir until combined well. Gently crack an egg into the water and let it poach until it becomes solid but the yolk looks like it would still run if released, 2 to 3 minutes. Poach the eggs one at a time for the best results. Using two large mixing spoons, delicately pull each egg when it is poached, setting each one on a plate on the side.

Place a fish cake on each plate. Pour ¼ of the sauce over each fish cake. Carefully place a poached egg on top of each fish cake. Garnish with the remaining parsley, lemon wedges, and a tiny sprinkle of the remaining ½ tablespoon paprika on top.

Store the fish cakes, sauce, and eggs in the refrigerator in separate airtight containers for 1 to 2 days, but they're best if eaten immediately when freshly made.

DEATHLY HALLOWS PULL-APART TEATIME BREAD

When prop makers originally designed the Resurrection Stone for *Harry Potter and the Half-Blood Prince*, they were unaware the Deathly Hallows should be etched upon it. Luckily, the seventh book came out before the design was finished, establishing the symbol.

This unique bread evokes the three components of the sign of the Deathly Hallows: Mini cheesy pull-apart breads, with a hint of onion, are arranged in the shape of a triangle, referencing the Cloak of Invisibility. The straight line of the Elder Wand is created with fresh thyme and rosemary. And the circle for the Resurrection Stone is formed by a tomato dipping sauce served in a round dish in the center.

The bread is served in individual portions, with a serving for each guest formed in a triangle shape. This serving arrangement is similar to pull-apart cupcakes, except these teatime bites are savory. This can be presented on a tea tray by itself, either on the table or on a side buffet.

FOR THE PULL-APART BREAD TRIANGLE

Three 8-ounce packages frozen crescent rolls, thawed

1 cup mini mozzarella cheese balls

½ cup grated Parmesan cheese

½ cup butter, melted

1 tablespoon diced red onion

1 teaspoon chopped fresh rosemary

1 tablespoon chopped fresh oregano leaves

¼ teaspoon salt

¼ teaspoon freshly ground black peppercorns

1 egg white

TO MAKE THE PULL-APART BREAD TRIANLE

Preheat the oven to 350°F. Line a 9-by-12-inch baking sheet with parchment paper.

Cut the dough into 1-inch pieces, and place in a large bowl. Add the mozzarella, Parmesan cheese, butter, onion, rosemary, oregano, salt, and peppercorns, and stir 3 or 4 times until combined well and the pieces of dough are covered in the melted butter thoroughly.

Arrange the dough mixture on the prepared baking sheet in the outline of a large triangle. Beat the egg white lightly in a small bowl, and use a pastry brush to cover the bread with the egg white.

Bake until golden brown all around, especially around the edges, about 45 minutes. Remove from the oven and place the bread on a cheese board, cutting board, or large platter. Leave the oven on.

CONTINUED ON PAGE 96

CONTINUED FROM PAGE 95

FOR THE TOMATO SAUCE

8 large vine-ripened tomatoes, chopped into 1-inch pieces

4½ ounces tomato paste

½ cup extra-virgin olive oil

½ cup chopped fresh oregano leaves

½ teaspoon finely chopped rosemary

2 garlic cloves, minced

1 teaspoon granulated sugar

¼ teaspoon pink Himalayan sea salt

¼ teaspoon freshly ground multicolor peppercorns

FOR THE GARNISH

2 long sprigs fresh rosemary with the needles still on

1 tablespoon grated Parmesan cheese

1 teaspoon finely chopped fresh rosemary

1 teaspoon chopped fresh oregano leaves

¼ teaspoon red pepper flakes

TO MAKE THE TOMATO SAUCE

In a large bowl, combine the tomatoes, tomato paste, oil, oregano, rosemary, garlic, sugar, salt, and peppercorns. Stir 3 or 4 times, until blended well and coated in the oil.

Place the mixture into a roasting pan, and roast until the skins have loosened from the tomatoes, about 45 minutes. Stir after 30 minutes.

Remove from the oven, and use a spoon to mash down the tomatoes and stir everything several times.

Place a round clear glass dish in the middle of the bread triangle on the cheese board and fill it with the tomato sauce for dipping the bread. Place a long sprig of rosemary in a vertical line over the tomato sauce, ensuring that the rosemary extends from top to bottom of the bread triangle, in the center. Garnish with sprinkles of Parmesan cheese, rosemary, oregano, and red pepper flakes.

Store the tomato sauce in the refrigerator in an airtight container for 2 to 3 days. Store the bread at room temperature in an airtight container for 2 to 3 days.

"THE ELDER WAND. THE RESURRECTION STONE. THE CLOAK OF INVISIBILITY. TOGETHER, THEY MAKE UP THE DEATHLY HALLOWS. TOGETHER, THEY MAKE ONE THE MASTER OF DEATH."

—Xenophilius Lovegood

Harry Potter and the Deathly Hallows – Part 1

GREAT HALL TREACLE AND PINOT NOIR-ROASTED TURKEY DRUMSTICKS

As Ron Weasley savors the welcome feast in the Great Hall during his first year at Hogwarts in *Harry Potter and the Sorcerer's Stone*, he gobbles a pair of roast drumsticks two-handed style with gusto. Finishing those, he goes in for a third but is put off when Nearly Headless Nick's nearly headless head rises from the platter.

These turkey legs are basted with a hearty pinot noir wine heated with fresh sage, star anise, multicolored peppercorns, and a flavor Harry Potter adores—treacle!

The feasts served in the Great Hall throughout the Harry Potter films were "catered" by the props department under the advisement of director Chris Columbus, who wanted to use real food. But as very little food was actually eaten while filming, it became less and less inviting under the hot lights. After this, feast foods were typically created from molded resin.

FOR THE DRUMSTICKS

4 tablespoons extra-virgin olive oil, divided

8 turkey drumsticks

½ teaspoon pink Himalayan sea salt, divided

½ teaspoon freshly ground multicolor peppercorns, divided

> "I KNOW YOU. YOU'RE NEARLY HEADLESS NICK!"
>
> —Ron Weasley
>
> *Harry Potter and the Sorcerer's Stone*

TO MAKE THE DRUMSTICKS

Preheat the oven to 375°F.

In a large skillet over medium heat, heat 2 tablespoons oil. Place the drumsticks in the skillet, sprinkle ¼ teaspoon each of salt and pepper over them, and brown them well on both sides, 8 to 10 minutes each side. Sprinkle the remaining ¼ teaspoon of salt and ¼ teaspoon pepper on the bottom side after they are flipped.

Grease a Dutch oven or roasting pan with the remaining 2 tablespoons oil. Place the cooked drumsticks in the greased pan.

CONTINUED ON PAGE 98

CONTINUED FROM PAGE 97

FOR THE BLACK TREACLE AND PINOT NOIR BASTE

1 cup pinot noir wine

1 cup chopped fresh sage, divided

½ cup honey

¼ cup brown sugar

¼ cup black treacle or molasses

1 teaspoon chopped ginger

2 garlic cloves, minced

1 bay leaf

1 star anise

½ teaspoon dried juniper berries

¼ teaspoon dry mustard

¼ teaspoon pink Himalayan sea salt

¼ teaspoon freshly ground multicolor peppercorns

1 pinch ground cloves

TO MAKE THE BLACK TREACLE AND PINOT NOIR BASTE

In a small saucepan over high heat, combine the wine, ½ cup sage, honey, brown sugar, treacle, ginger, garlic, bay leaf, star anise, juniper berries, mustard, salt, peppercorns, and clove. Bring to a boil. Reduce the heat to medium and simmer, stirring occasionally, for 45 minutes. Using a handheld fine-mesh strainer, strain the baste liquid into a large mixing bowl to remove the bay leaf, star anise, and juniper berries.

Using a pastry brush, coat the drumsticks with a thick layer of the black treacle and pinot noir baste.

Roast the drumsticks in the oven, uncovered, until the internal temperature of the meat is 165°F, 1½ to 2 hours. Flip the drumsticks after the first 45 minutes, and generously coat the top of the drumsticks with additional baste; repeat after 30 minutes more.

Arrange the drumsticks on a large platter, sprinkle with the remaining ½ cup sage, and serve.

Store in the refrigerator in an airtight container for 2 to 3 days.

BOWTRUCKLE ISLAND BUTTER BOARD

As their friendship grows, Newt Scamander takes a forlorn Leta Lestrange to Bowtruckle Island on the Black Lake in order to cheer her up in *Fantastic Beasts: The Crimes of Grindelwald*. He shows her the family of Bowtruckles that live in a bushy-topped tree, shy but clever creatures with the appearance of a walking arrangement of twigs and leaves.

This particular butter board gives tribute to Bowtruckle Island's inhabitants with leafy, chopped broccoli tops; bits of crispy bacon; herbs over the base of softened butter, plus a drizzle of honey for the sweetness Newt offers Leta during their school years. Toasted almonds are sprinkled evenly over the board to add another savory layer. The board is served with bite-size pieces of thinly sliced raisin bread toast points or crackers at your discretion, presented on a single tea tray.

FOR THE TOASTED ALMONDS

½ cup slivered almonds

1 tablespoon extra-virgin olive oil

¼ teaspoon salt

¼ teaspoon freshly ground black pepper

FOR THE BUTTER BOARD

8 ounces butter, softened

1 tablespoon honey

1 cup steamed broccoli tops, dried well

¼ cup crispy bacon bits

1 tablespoon raisins

¼ cup radicchio lettuce, chiffonade

FOR THE PRESENTATION

Raisin bread or crackers

TO MAKE THE TOASTED ALMONDS

Preheat the oven to 350°F. Line a baking sheet with parchment paper.

In a small bowl, toss the almonds in the oil, salt, and pepper. Arrange the almonds on the prepared baking sheet. Make sure the almonds do not overlap so that they can all brown. Bake for 20 minutes, stirring after 10 minutes. Remove from the oven, and set aside to cool.

TO MAKE THE BUTTER BOARD

Use a butter knife to spread the butter evenly across a board or serving platter. Drizzle the honey on top. Arrange the broccoli, bacon, raddichio, and raisins evenly across the butter and honey. Sprinkle the toasted almonds evenly across the board.

Serve with toasted raisin bread or crackers.

Store the butter board in the refrigerator in an airtight container for 1 to 2 days, but it's best if eaten immediately. Store the bread at room temperature in an airtight container for 2 to 3 days.

"GOOD GRAVY!" MINI MEAT LOAF TEA SANDWICHES

The 1920s contributed heaps of slang to the American language: "Know your onions" (know what's up), "juice joint" (a speakeasy), and "sounds like berries to me!" (that's good!). Another was "good gravy!" a way of expressing surprise or annoyance without using profanity, commonly used in New York City.

When Queenie Goldstein tries to leave MACUSA with Newt, Jacob, and Tina hidden in Newt's case, she runs into her boss, Abernathy, who wonders why she's leaving so early. Queenie fakes being sick, but he continues his questioning—what's in the case? Brilliantly, she replies, "Ladies' things." This upsets Abernathy, but Queenie makes him jittery anyway, unnerving him even more, so he replies with the expression "good gravy!" when she offers to let him take a look.

Inspired by this amusing scene, there's no better way to enjoy a bite-size meat loaf sandwich than with a ketchup-based "good gravy."

FOR THE MEAT LOAF

2 tablespoons butter, divided

2 pounds ground beef

½ cup diced red onion

2 large eggs

2 garlic cloves, minced

2 tablespoons finely chopped fresh parsley

1 cup plain breadcrumbs

⅓ cup whole milk

1 teaspoon pink Himalayan sea salt

½ teaspoon freshly ground peppercorns

½ teaspoon dry mustard

½ teaspoon ground paprika

24 mini sandwich buns

FOR THE "GOOD GRAVY!"

4 cups ketchup

2 tablespoons apple cider vinegar

1 teaspoon paprika

1 garlic clove, minced

½ teaspoon freshly ground multicolor peppercorns

¼ teaspoon pink Himalayan sea salt

Note ✦ The secret for the best meat loaf is to mix the ingredients well. And, like with any classic meat loaf, this is even better the next day or even 2 days after making it.

TO MAKE THE MEAT LOAF

Preheat the oven to 375°F. Using 1 tablespoon butter, grease a 9-by-5-inch loaf pan.

In a large bowl, combine the remaining 1 tablespoon butter, ground beef, onion, eggs, garlic, parsley, breadcrumbs, milk, salt, peppercorns, mustard, and paprika. Using your hands, mix the ingredients together well, for 2 to 3 minutes.

Press the meat loaf mixture into the loaf pan, and bake until the edges become browned all around and pull away from the sides of the pan, 40 to 45 minutes.

Remove from the oven, and set aside for a few minutes. When the meat loaf is no longer too hot to touch, slice it into 1-inch-thick pieces.

TO MAKE THE "GOOD GRAVY!"

Combine the ketchup, vinegar, paprika, garlic, peppercorns, and salt in a mixing bowl, and stir until well combined.

To make a sandwich, place a piece of meat loaf and a tablespoon of the "Good Gravy!" between two of the mini sandwich buns.

Store the meat loaf in the refrigerator in an airtight container for 3 to 4 days. Store the bread at room temperature in an airtight container for 3 to 4 days.

"OH! GOOD GRAVY. NO!"

—Abernathy

Fantastic Beasts and Where to Find Them

"WILL YOU STOP EATING? YOUR BEST
FRIEND IS MISSING!"

"TURN AROUND. YOU LUNATIC."

—Hermione Granger and Ron Weasley

Harry Potter and the Half-Blood Prince

RON WEASLEY'S TEATIME RASPBERRY GELATIN TREATS

When Harry Potter doesn't initially show up in the Great Hall after everyone else has departed the Hogwarts Express in *Harry Potter and the Half-Blood Prince*, Hermione takes out her concern by smacking Ron as he mindlessly shovels spoonfuls of a red gelatin dish into his mouth.

Actress Emma Watson (Hermione) always thought that Hermione and Ron would end up together. "I always thought there was a tension between them," says Watson, "and the reason they argue so much, and find each other so annoying, is they were so hyperaware of each other because they fancied each other." Watson approved of the relationship, though. "They're so wrong for each other, but so right."

Harry finally turns up, and so, inspired by this sequence, this dish is a raspberry-flavored layered gelatin salad made in a mold. Layers include a basil cream cheese spread and a salty pretzel base that Ron surely wouldn't be able to stop eating.

FOR THE GELATIN

1 tablespoon butter, for greasing the muffin pan

12 ounces strawberry or raspberry gelatin

2 cups cold water

One 10-ounce package frozen strawberries or raspberries

FOR THE PRETZEL MIXTURE

2 cups chopped pretzels

½ cup butter, softened

3 tablespoons granulated sugar

NOTE ✦ For a gluten-free teatime treat, make this without the pretzel base.

TO MAKE THE GELATIN

Use the butter to grease the cavities of a 12-cup muffin pan.

In a medium saucepan over medium heat, bring 2 cups water to a boil. Add the gelatin, and stir just until dissolved, 2 to 3 minutes. Add in the cold water, and stir. Add the frozen berries, and stir. Pour the mixture into the prepared muffin pan. Allow at least ½ inch on top for the basil cream cheese spread and pretzels. Chill in the refrigerator for at least 4 hours.

TO MAKE THE PRETZEL MIXTURE

Blend the pretzels, butter, and sugar in a food processor until the pretzels become coarse and the mixture becomes a doughlike consistency, about 5 pulses. Place the pretzel mixture in a small bowl, and set aside until time to assemble. Clean the food processor to prepare it for making the basil cream cheese layer.

CONTINUED ON PAGE 106

CONTINUED FROM PAGE 105

FOR THE BASIL CREAM CHEESE SPREAD

12 ounces cream cheese, softened

1 cup granulated sugar

One 8-ounce carton whipped cream topping

1 handful fresh basil

TO MAKE THE BASIL CREAM CHEESE SPREAD

Pulse the cream cheese, sugar, and whipped cream in the food processor until well combined, about 3 pulses.

When the gelatin is completely set, spread a thin layer of cream cheese mixture on top of each gelatin, followed by a layer of the pretzel mix.

Use 2 large mixing spoons to delicately pull each of the molded gelatin cups out of the cavities of the muffin pan. If the gelatin does not easily pull away from the muffin pan, dip the bottom of the pan in a sink filled with hot water for 2 seconds.

Garnish with the fresh basil, and serve each individual gelatin cup on a plate, pretzel side down.

Store in the refrigerator in an airtight container for 2 to 3 days.

HAGRID'S BUTTERNUT SQUASH MINI TARTLETS WITH CRISPY BACON AND SAGE

When Harry, Ron, and Hermione visit Hagrid's hut in *Harry Potter and the Prisoner of Azkaban*, his garden is filled with gorgeous, bright orange pumpkins, which are one of many types of squash. And Hagrid may be growing other squashes there, such as butternut squash, with its, yes, buttery and nutty taste, used in this dish.

Hagrid's hut and its pumpkin patch were filmed in Scotland for *Prisoner of Azkaban*. Production designer Stuart Craig found the gorgeous backdrop and ample space to be gratifying—until filming began and it rained continuously! However, he did appreciate the different, "serious energy" the rain clouds and shadows brought to the look of the sequence. Not surprisingly, it was one of the last times the crew shot extensively on location.

These rectangular-shaped puff pastry tartlets are topped with thin pieces of butternut squash tossed in a honey glaze, drops of cream cheese, fresh sage, and bits of crispy fried bacon to create a dish Hagrid would surely be proud to serve visitors to his hut.

½ butternut squash, peeled and cut into quarters (thin pie-shaped pieces)

2 tablespoons extra-virgin olive oil

1 tablespoon honey

1 pinch pink Himalayan sea salt

1 dash freshly ground multicolor peppercorns

2 tablespoons chopped fresh sage

½ package frozen pastry dough

1 egg

Preheat the oven to 350°F. Line a baking sheet with parchment paper.

In a large mixing bowl, combine the squash, oil, honey, salt, peppercorns, and sage. Toss for 1 minute, and then set aside to marinate.

Cut the pastry dough into 2-by-4-inch rectangles, and arrange the pieces on the prepared baking sheet. The dough will yield about 6 to 8 rectangles. Whisk the egg in a small bowl and use a pastry brush to paint the egg on each of the pastry pieces.

CONTINUED ON PAGE 109

"COME IN. I'VE JUST MADE A POT OF TEA."

—Rubeus Hagrid

Harry Potter and the Chamber of Secrets

CONTINUED FROM PAGE 107

2 tablespoons cream cheese

2 strips bacon, baked until crispy and chopped

Note: For a vegetarian option, make these without bacon.

Place 3 tablespoons of the squash and sage mixture on top of each of the pieces of pastry dough. Sprinkle tiny bits of cream cheese and bacon on the top of each pastry piece. Drizzle the remaining oil from the squash and sage mixture over each tartlet.

Leave the top open, with no top crust.

Bake until each pastry piece is baked all the way through and brown on the tops and edges, 40 to 45 minutes.

Remove the tartlets from the oven, and serve warm.

Store in the refrigerator in an airtight container for 3 to 4 days.

AUNT PETUNIA'S TEATIME HAM BITES

In *Harry Potter and the Chamber of Secrets*, the Dursleys host the affluent Masons for dinner, and Vernon is adamant the evening goes well. "He doesn't want anything strange happening that the neighbors might see," Richard Griffiths (Vernon) said. "The Dursleys want to be ordinary, average, and normal, and Harry Potter prevents the possibility of all this, which is terrifying to them." Petunia has done her best to prepare a dinner that will please their guests, but Vernon's worst fears are realized when the dinner ends in disaster.

These ham bites would be a perfect dish to serve no matter the occasion but are a great item for a high tea. The warm meatballs are drizzled with a tangy glaze made from fruits such as pineapples or peaches, and Scotch whisky. Serve them with a small piece of pineapple, a maraschino cherry, and a sprig of fresh pineapple mint. Arrange these on a tea tray, but separate them from other foods so that the light juice on each meatball does not mix with other items.

FOR THE MEATBALLS

1 pound freshly ground ham

1 pound freshly ground beef

1 cup crushed crackers

3 eggs

1 cup whole milk

1 red bell pepper, diced

2 tablespoons dry mustard

3 garlic cloves, minced

2 tablespoons fresh marjoram leaves, divided

½ teaspoon pink Himalayan sea salt

½ teaspoon freshly ground peppercorns

FOR THE GLAZE

5 ounces peach, pineapple, or elderberry preserves

1 tablespoon Scotch whisky

1 tablespoon chicken or vegetable stock

FOR THE CONDIMENTS

1 cup pineapple jam

1 cup peach jam

1 cup ketchup

Note ✦ Ask the butcher to grind the ham and beef and mix it together.

"NOT NOW. POPKIN. FOR WHEN THE MASONS ARRIVE."

—Petunia Dursley

Harry Potter and the Chamber of Secrets

TO MAKE THE MEATBALLS

Preheat the oven to 350°F. Line a baking sheet with parchment paper.

In the bowl of a stand mixer or in a large mixing bowl using your hands, combine the ham, beef, crackers, eggs, milk, red bell pepper, mustard, garlic, 1 tablespoon marjoram leaves, the salt, and peppercorns. Mix until combined well, but be careful not to overmix so that the meatballs do not become overly dense.

Use a small ice-cream scoop to create 1-inch balls. Using your hands, roll each ball until it is smooth all around.

Arrange the meatballs on the prepared baking sheet 1 inch apart. Bake until the edges become browned, about 1 hour.

TO MAKE THE GLAZE

In a small saucepan over medium-high heat, combine the preserves, Scotch, and stock, and bring to a boil. Reduce the heat to medium and simmer, stirring occasionally, until blended well, about 15 minutes.

Remove the meatballs from the oven, drizzle with glaze, and sprinkle with the remaining 1 tablespoon marjoram leaves. Serve on a platter with bamboo picks alongside three small clear glass bowls filled with pineapple jam, peach jam, and ketchup.

Store in the refrigerator in an airtight container for 3 to 4 days.

TINA GOLDSTEIN'S BITE-SIZE HOT DOGS WITH HONEY MUSTARD SAUCE

In *Fantastic Beasts and Where to Find Them*, Newt Scamander meets the former Auror Tina Goldstein on the steps of Steen National Bank while she watches Mary Lou Barebone, head of the New Salem Philanthropic Society, campaign to expose and wipe out wizarding kind in a fiery speech. Tina watches, eating a hot dog, which leaves a smear of mustard on her lip.

As one passion of Tina's sister, Queenie, is cooking, graphic artists Miraphora Mina and Eduardo Lima filled the Goldstein apartment with cookbooks, including one on how to cook like a No-Maj, called *Franks and Human Beans*. The book just happens to have a recipe for apple strudel in it. In addition to that recipe and others in the book, Mina and Lima provided the labels for the flour and sugar products used when Queenie bakes.

These savory mini beef hot dogs are served in little golden-brown buns, with a honey mustard sauce. Napkins are a must, so as not to end up with mustard on your lip like Tina!

FOR THE MINI HOT DOGS

1 pound frozen bread dough

1¾ pounds mini hot dogs

Note ✦ For a gluten-free savory teatime treat, offer mini hot dogs without the bun, presented on a bamboo cocktail stick.

FOR THE HONEY MUSTARD

2 tablespoons dry mustard powder

1 tablespoon mustard seeds

3 tablespoons honey

¼ teaspoon apple cider vinegar

½ teaspoon turmeric

¼ teaspoon pink Himalayan sea salt

¼ teaspoon freshly ground black peppercorns

> "ER. YOU'VE GOT SOMETHING ON YOUR–"
>
> —Newt Scamander to Tina Goldstein
>
> *Fantastic Beasts and Where to Find Them*

TO MAKE THE MINI HOT DOGS

Preheat the oven to 350°F. Line two baking sheets with parchment paper.

Take the bread dough out of the freezer to thaw. When the dough has thawed, cut 2-inch pieces, and roll them into oval shapes. The dough will yield 18 to 20 mini hot dog buns.

Place 18 of the bread dough ovals on one of the prepared baking sheets and bake until golden brown around the edges and lightly browned on top, 50 to 60 minutes.

Place the mini hot dogs on the second baking sheet, and bake until dark brown all around, about 40 minutes.

Remove the mini breads and the mini hot dogs from the oven, and set aside to cool for 2 to 3 minutes.

Use a serrated knife to cut the mini breads horizontally on one side. Do not cut all the way through.

TO MAKE THE HONEY MUSTARD

Combine the mustard powder, mustard seeds, honey, vinegar, turmeric, salt, and peppercorns in a large mixing bowl, and use a spoon to mix together well.

Place a mini hot dog in each bun, and top with a line of honey mustard.

Store the hot dogs in the refrigerator in an airtight container for 2 to 3 days. Store the mustard in the refrigerator in an airtight container for 2 to 3 weeks. Store the bread at room temperature in an airtight container for 3 to 4 days.

RON WEASLEY'S SAVORY ESCARGOT-STUFFED MUSHROOMS

When Ron Weasley crashes into the Whomping Willow at Hogwarts in *Harry Potter and the Chamber of Secrets*, he breaks his wand. He fastens it with Spello-Tape, but the wand is still wonky. Later, defending Hermione after Draco insults her, Ron casts "Eat slugs!" but the spell backfires and Ron ends up expectorating a trio of gastropods.

That scene was one of Rupert Grint's (Ron) favorites. "I had to put these giant slugs in my mouth and then spit them out with all this lovely goo," says Grint. The slime of the three plastic slugs used, which were named Monty, Vincent, and Ethel, were flavored with chocolate, lemon, orange, and peppermint.

Escargots are a French delicacy that taste a bit like mussels. Arrange these escargot-stuffed mushrooms in classic French escargot plates, with a bamboo pick in each so that guests can eat them in one bite.

- 2 tablespoons extra-virgin olive oil
- 7 ounces canned escargot, rinsed, drained, and finely chopped
- 4 ounces crab, fresh or canned, drained
- 2 tablespoons diced red onion
- 1 tablespoon diced fresh red bell pepper
- 1 tablespoon plain breadcrumbs
- ¼ teaspoon dry mustard
- 1 cup chopped fresh parsley tops (no stems), divided
- ½ cup pinot grigio or other dry white wine
- 1 fresh lemon
- ½ teaspoon freshly ground multicolor peppercorns
- ¼ teaspoon pink Himalayan sea salt
- 1 tablespoon butter, room temperature
- 24 medium and large button mushrooms
- 2 tablespoons grated Parmesan cheese
- 1 lemon, cut into ¼-inch-thick wedges

Preheat the oven to 350°F.

In a frying pan over medium heat, heat the oil. Add the escargot, crab, onion, bell pepper, breadcrumbs, mustard, ⅔ cup parsley, the wine, juice from ½ the lemon, pepper, and salt. Use a spoon to combine the ingredients together well. Cook, stirring occasionally, for about 30 minutes.

With the butter, grease a 9-inch pie plate or 8-inch-square baking dish.

Brush off the mushrooms to remove any soil, and pull the stem out from the center of each mushroom. Arrange the mushrooms in the prepared baking dish, top side down, so that the openings are facing up.

Use a spoon to stuff the escargot mixture into each mushroom cap. Stuff as much of the mixture into each mushroom as the mushroom will hold. Capacity will vary with size of each mushroom.

Sprinkle the mushrooms with the Parmesan cheese, and bake until the stuffing and the mushrooms become baked together and the mushrooms become much darker, 30 to 40 minutes.

Remove from the oven and serve hot, sprinkled with the remaining ⅓ cup fresh parsley and lemon wedges.

Store in the refrigerator in an airtight container for 1 to 2 days, but they're best if eaten immediately when fresh and warm.

"EAT SLUGS!"

—Ron Weasley

Harry Potter and the Chamber of Secrets

KOWALSKI BAKERY'S BUTTERY TEATIME WITCH HATS WITH MAGICAL HERBAL BROOMSTICKS

When Jacob Kowalski opens his bakery after the memory of his time in the wizarding world is Obliviated, in *Fantastic Beasts and Where to Find Them*, it's stocked with breads, cakes, and something much more unusual: pastry versions of beasts the Muggle world has never seen before. "There's this subliminal sort of memory that's coming out in what he's baking," says prop modeler Pierre Bohanna. And so, pastry versions of Demiguises, Nifflers, Erumpents, and Occamys are sold alongside the rolls and paczki. "Obviously they're not *real* breads," Bohanna adds about the synthetic creatures cast in molds, "but they're beautiful artworks."

Serve these very real, witch hat-shaped breads on individual small plates with a dollop of heart-shaped butter, using the herbal "broomstick" to spread the butter. The broomsticks, inspired by Harry's state-of-the-art Firebolt broomstick, are a mix of thyme, dill, and tarragon on a "handle" made of rosemary. The herbs add fresh flavors to both the butter and bread.

FOR THE BEAST BREADS

1 pound frozen breadstick dough, thawed

1 cup all-purpose flour

4 black olives

FOR THE HERBAL BROOMSTICKS

Four 4-inch sprigs fresh rosemary

Four 2-inch sprigs fresh tarragon

Four 2-inch sprigs fresh dill

Four 2-inch sprigs fresh oregano

Sixteen 5-inch sprigs fresh chives

TO MAKE THE BEAST BREADS

Preheat the oven to 350°F.

Place a piece of parchment paper in the base of 2 aluminum baking pans with 2-inch-high sides.

Sprinkle some flour on the countertop to work on the dough.

Using a knife, cut the bread dough into thirds to create rectangles. Pull one end into a curved point. Make a small ½-inch slit in the other end and pull the two sides of the cut into a hat brim shape as desired. Use a sharp knife to cut some slits into the hat body for texture. Brush with butter and bake for 15 to 30 minutes.

Remove the breads from the oven, leaving them in their pans to cool on the countertop.

CONTINUED ON PAGE 119

CONTINUED FROM PAGE 117

FOR THE GARLIC BUTTER SAUCE

1 cup butter

1 garlic clove, minced

1 tablespoon fresh tarragon leaves

1 tablespoon chopped fresh dill

1 tablespoon chopped fresh oregano

1 tablespoon chopped fresh chives

KOWALSKI
QUALITY
BAKED
GOODS.
EST. 1927   443

When the breads have cooled enough to touch, divide the bread among 4 plates, and place an herbal broomstick alongside the bread on the plate.

TO MAKE THE HERBAL BROOMSTICKS

Strip the needles from the sprigs of rosemary, leaving the top ⅓ in place. Arrange one sprig each of the tarragon, dill, and oregano around the top part of the rosemary.

Place the chives in a damp paper towel and microwave for 20 seconds. Divide the chives into 4 equal parts, and tie them around the herbs to secure them at the top of the rosemary sprigs. Serve a broomstick on each plate to use as a brush to apply the butter to the bread.

Store the breads at room temperature in an airtight container for 3 to 4 days. Store the butter in the refrigerator in an airtight container for 6 to 7 days. Store the herbs in the refrigerator in an airtight container for 2 to 3 days.

TO MAKE THE GARLIC BUTTER SAUCE

Just before serving, melt the butter in a glass bowl in the microwave. Stir in the garlic, tarragon, dill, oregano, and chives and mix well. Serve alongside the breads.

> "WHERE DO YOU GET YOUR IDEAS FROM, MR. KOWALSKI?"
>
> "I DON'T KNOW. I DON'T KNOW—THEY JUST COME!"
>
> —Female Customer to Jacob Kowalski
>
> *Fantastic Beasts and Where to Find Them*

MOLLY WEASLEY'S BANGERS AND ROASTED TOMATO QUICHE BITES

Actress Julie Walters calls her character "a mother who happens to be a witch. She's a sweet person, and the most real of them in so many ways," she adds. Walters maintains that no matter what is happening around her, "she's a force for good, a force for all the good stuff in the world: love, family, and what's good about humanity."

These small teatime quiches, which can be eaten in two bites, are inspired by classic English breakfasts Mrs. Weasley might make for her family. Although quiche is often considered a French dish, the name is actually German for "cake." This popular brunch item is extremely adaptable, with a custardy base of milk, cream, and eggs. Then it's all about the add-ins! English breakfast bangers (encased sausages) and roasted tomatoes are a custom in every British household.

FOR THE ROASTED TOMATOES

5 large vine-ripened tomatoes

3 tablespoons extra-virgin olive oil

2 garlic cloves, minced

1 teaspoon coarse salt

¼ teaspoon freshly ground black peppercorns

NOTE ✦ Almost any shredded soft cheese will work well; however, Swiss cheese will provide the most authentic flavor of a classic French quiche.

For a gluten-free option, these can also be made without the crusts.

TO MAKE THE ROASTED TOMATOES

Preheat the oven to 350°F.

Chop the tomatoes into quarters. Place the tomatoes on a baking sheet, and drizzle with the olive oil. Sprinkle with the garlic, salt, and pepper. Roast for 30 to 40 minutes, stirring after the first 20 minutes.

Remove the tomatoes from the oven, and set on a plate lined with paper towels on the counter to cool. Place paper towel on top of the tomatoes, and gently press to absorb some of the oil.

CONTINUED ON PAGE 123

"COME ON. HARRY. TIME FOR A SPOT OF BREAKFAST. HERE WE ARE. HARRY. TUCK IN. THAT'S IT. THERE WE GO."

—Molly Weasley

Harry Potter and the Chamber of Secrets

CONTINUED FROM PAGE 121

FOR THE QUICHE

4 frozen piecrusts

One 16-ounce package Polish sausage (kielbasa) or other sausage links

8 large eggs

2 cups milk

1 cup heavy whipping cream

1 cup grated Swiss cheese, divided

1 cup grated Parmesan cheese

2 teaspoons dry mustard

½ cup diced red onion

1 cup chopped fresh basil, divided

¼ teaspoon freshly ground black pepper

1 tablespoon butter, for greasing the pan

TO MAKE THE QUICHE

Remove the piecrusts from the freezer and set them on the countertop until thawed, about 30 minutes. When the piecrusts are thawed, use a 2-inch round cookie cutter to cut the dough into 25 round pieces.

In a large skillet over medium heat, brown the sausage links, 20 to 30 minutes. Turn the sausages over when they are brown on one side, about halfway through cooking.

In a large mixing bowl, use a fork to break the egg yolks and gently beat the eggs, 1 to 2 minutes; add the milk, cream, ½ cup Swiss cheese, Parmesan cheese, mustard, onion, ⅞ cup basil, and the pepper, and use a large spoon to mix together. Combine thoroughly. Cut the browned sausages into ¼-inch round pieces, and add to the mixing bowl. Add the roasted tomatoes. Mix well.

Use the butter to grease the rounds of two 12-capacity cupcake pans. Place one of the piecrust rounds in each of the cupcake pan cavities; use your fingers to shape the dough so that it covers the inside of each round. Pat around the edges at the top to smooth out the crust all around. Use a fork to pierce holes in the bottom of each round of piecrust dough.

Place 1 cup of the mixture into each round in the cupcake pans, making sure that each type of ingredient is in every round. Sprinkle the remaining ½ cup Swiss cheese on top.

Bake until the quiches become the consistency of custard and the edges are dark brown, 40 to 45 minutes.

Sprinkle with remaining ⅛ cup basil before serving.

Store in the refrigerator in an airtight container for 3 to 4 days.

CHAPTER THREE

TEATIME CANDIES, SNACKS, AND TAKE-HOME GIFTS

FROGGY FANCIES

Chocolate Frogs are an extremely popular wizarding treat. The five-sided box created to house the jumping confection was designed by graphics department artist Ruth Winick, based upon input by production designer Stuart Craig. "Stuart drew the shape of a pentagon and said I should think 'classical,'" says Winick. She looked at Gothic architecture as a source for the packaging. On the top of the Chocolate Frog box are images that evoke the trefoil windows that are the Gothic style of Hogwarts castle. The graphics department was also responsible for adding ingredients, slogans, and establishing dates of the Honeydukes candies.

The melted chocolate here is sweetened by blackberry flavoring for a warming lift. Thankfully, these treats inspired by the Chocolate Frogs sold by Honeydukes in *Harry Potter and the Sorcerer's Stone* won't jump out a window before you can eat them!

2 cups chocolate chips

2 tablespoons rice crisp cereal

1 teaspoon blackberry extract

SPECIALTY TOOLS

1 sheet frog-shaped plastic candy molds

Cooking spray

Note ✦ For a vegan option, use dairy-free chocolate chips.

In a double boiler over medium-low heat, or in a microwave-safe bowl in the microwave, melt the chocolate. If using the microwave, microwave for 1 minute, stirring after 30 seconds. Add the rice crisp cereal and the blackberry extract, and stir well to combine thoroughly. The mixture will become stiff, like the consistency of cookie dough.

Spray cooking spray inside the frog molds. Wipe away excess with a soft cloth.

Using your fingers, place the chocolate mixture into each of the frog molds. Spread the chocolate throughout each of the molds, ensuring that the chocolate is the same thickness all over. Press in around the edges so that all of the chocolate is inside the mold. Push down on top of each mold that is filled with chocolate to flatten and smooth out the tops.

CONTINUED ON PAGE 128

"THESE AREN'T REAL FROGS, ARE THEY?"

"IT'S JUST A SPELL."

—Harry Potter to Ron Weasley

Harry Potter and the Sorcerer's Stone

CONTINUED FROM PAGE 127

Place the molds in the refrigerator until the chocolate is firm enough to remove it from the molds without breaking, about 4 hours.

Once set, carefully pull the chocolate from the molds. Arrange the frogs on a serving platter. Create a platter with a mix of the Divination Dream Bar Tea Treats (page 20), Feverless Fudge Tea Bites (page 129), Dumbledore's Elderberry Tea Pastilles (page 143), Dementors Mini Chocolate Teatime Treats (page 136), Disenchantment Tea Candies (page 133), or Chocolate Flying Keys (page 139).

Store at room temperature in an airtight container for 5 to 6 days.

✦ BEHIND THE MAGIC ✦

The label for Chocolate Frogs includes information that 70 percent of a Chocolate Frog contains the finest *croakoa*—a mash-up of "croak" and "cacao," aka "cocoa bean," the seed from which chocolate is made.

FEVERLESS FUDGE TEA BITES

In their fifth year at Hogwarts, Fred and George Weasley began a business selling the Skiving Snackbox, which contains candies that allow a student to feign illness to leave class, with the antidote on the other side of the candy. But students were not the only targets. One of the box's bestsellers—Fever Fudge—was used on Argus Filch when he was caught spying on the newly created Dumbledore's Army in *Harry Potter and the Order of the Phoenix*.

When Fred and George leave Hogwarts to pursue careers as entrepreneurs, they establish a joke shop on Diagon Alley, in *Harry Potter and the Half-Blood Prince*. Weasleys' Wizard Wheezes sells fireworks, jokes, and sweets, including Fever Fudge. Prop makers used nearly eighty gallons of silicone in a variety of revolting colors to make the candies they sell.

These minty, chocolaty, marshmallowy *feverless* fudge bites won't cause the same reaction of Fever Fudge—just a smile and sigh at its sweet, bright flavor.

3 cups granulated sugar

¾ cup butter

⅔ cup evaporated milk

4 ounces mint chocolate chips

8 ounces milk chocolate chips

7 ounces marshmallow cream

1 cup mini marshmallows

1 teaspoon peppermint extract

1 tablespoon fresh chocolate mint leaves

"STEP UP, STEP UP! WE'VE GOT FAINTING FANCIES, NOSEBLEED NOUGAT, AND JUST IN TIME FOR SCHOOL, PUKING PASTILLES!"

—Fred and George Weasley

Harry Potter and the Half-Blood Prince

Place parchment paper in a 9-by-12-inch baking pan, ensuring that the paper goes up the sides of the pan. For thicker pieces of fudge, use an 8-inch-square baking dish.

In a medium saucepan over high heat, combine the sugar, butter, and evaporated milk. Bring to a rolling boil. Continue to boil for 4 minutes, stirring the mixture constantly. Remove from the heat. Use a spoon to quickly mix in the mint chocolate and milk chocolate chips. When the chocolates are thoroughly mixed in, add the marshmallow cream, and combine well. Add the mini marshmallows and peppermint extract, and stir well to combine, ensuring the peppermint flavor is incorporated well.

Pour the fudge mixture into the prepared baking pan. Set this aside to cool and firm up, about 4 hours. Cut the fudge into tiny pieces. Garnish with fresh mint leaves, chiffonade or whole, and serve on a small plate.

Store at room temperature in an airtight container for 2 to 3 weeks.

"YOUR GRANDFATHER KEPT PIGEONS? MINE
BRED OWLS. I USED TO LOVE FEEDING 'EM."

—Queenie Goldstein to Jacob Kowalski

Fantastic Beasts and Where to Find Them

GF, V ✦ YIELD: 18 TO 20
SERVINGS IN SMALL SNACK
CUPS; 4 TO 6 SERVINGS IN
CANNING JARS

GRANDFATHER GOLDSTEIN'S TEATIME OWL FOOD

After Queenie Goldstein rescues Newt, Tina, and Jacob from MACUSA headquarters, where the Director of Magical Security had imprisoned them, the quartet finds themselves regrouping on a New York rooftop that features a pigeon coop. Jacob's recollection from his past brings up a fond memory in Queenie.

Queenie and Tina Goldstein were orphaned at an early age, their parents having passed from dragon pox. "Tina and Queenie are each other's family," says Alison Sudol (Queenie). Though they may be opposites in personality and style, "It's very easy for Queenie to just love Tina. You don't need to prove how much you love somebody if you love them enough, and that's how I feel with Tina and Queenie."

This roasted fruit and nut snack inspired by the Goldstein sisters' grandfather includes ingredients that appeal to humans as well as owls. Serve this as a finger snack, or package them in canning jars to give to your guests to take home.

1 cup walnuts

1 cup almonds

1 cup cashews

1 cup freeze-dried strawberries

1 cup freeze-dried blueberries

½ cup dried mango, cut in ½-inch pieces

½ cup dried apricots, cut in ½-inch pieces

1 cup honey

1 tablespoon butter, melted

1 tablespoon fresh thyme leaves

¼ teaspoon flake salt

¼ teaspoon freshly ground multicolor peppercorns

Preheat the oven to 350°F. Line a baking sheet with parchment paper.

In a large bowl, combine the walnuts, almonds, cashews, strawberries, blueberries, mango, apricots, honey, butter, thyme, salt, and peppercorns, and stir until combined well.

Spread the mixture out on the prepared baking sheet. Roast until the strawberries start to become slightly dark around the edges, 20 to 25 minutes.

Remove from the oven and set aside to cool to room temperature.

Store at room temperature in an airtight container for 2 to 3 weeks.

DISENCHANTMENT TEA CANDIES

As Newt works with the beasts in his house in London in *Fantastic Beasts: The Crimes of Grindelwald*, he finds that Queenie Goldstein and Jacob Kowalski have let themselves in for a visit. But over dinner, Newt realizes that something is off with Jacob—he shakes salt on his hand instead of his food, and he toasts his engagement to Queenie by splashing a glass of champagne into his face!

"Jacob is being unnaturally jolly," says Dan Fogler. "I'm a little bit too happy. It turns out Queenie has put me under her spell." A very *specific* spell. When Newt performs the *Surgito* spell on Jacob to remove Queenie's love enchantment, a bright red heart appears above Jacob's head.

These heart-shaped jelly candies inspired by *Surgito* are made with raspberry tea. They can be set out in a candy dish, arranged among other teatime sweets on a tea tray, or packaged in a container for guests to take home.

4 ounces unflavored gelatin powder

3 ounces cherry, raspberry, or strawberry gelatin

1 cup cherry, raspberry, or strawberry jam

SPECIALTY TOOLS

2 candy molds with twelve 2-inch heart shapes or 1 candy mold with 24 heart shapes

Cooking spray

In a small saucepan over high heat, bring ½ cup water to a boil, and add the gelatin powder, cherry gelatin, and jam. Boil until thickened, about 4 minutes, stirring continuously.

Spray a heart-shaped candy mold with cooking spray. Wipe away any excess with a damp, soft cloth.

Use a small spoon to carefully fill each of the hearts.

Place in the refrigerator until the hearts set, about 1 hour.

Use a plastic knife to remove the hearts by putting the knife into the base of each heart and carefully and lightly pushing the knife around between the gelatin and the mold, and pulling the gelatin out of each mold.

Serve the hearts on a serving tray or place a few in small clear plastic candy bags, tied with ribbon, for guests to take home with them.

Store in the refrigerator in an airtight container for 5 to 6 days.

PICKLED "ASHWINDER" EGGS

As Newt pursues his missing beasts in *Fantastic Beasts and Where to Find Them*, Tina suggests he see Gnarlak, the goblin owner of The Blind Pig speakeasy, who trades in magical creatures and might have seen one. Newt realizes that he'll have to make it worth Gnarlak's while to get information, and so offers Galleons, a Lunascope, and finally a frozen Ashwinder egg, used most often in love potions.

"A guy in Gnarlak's position just knows how to make deals with every stratum," says Ron Perlman, who plays the seedy goblin, "be it the highest stations in government or the lowest form of criminality and nefariousness."

Pickled eggs are a common sight in drinking establishments; these hard-boiled eggs are pickled in white wine vinegar with bay leaves and juniper berries. Serve these in a shallow bowl or give each guest a few in a canning jar to take home with twine or ribbon tied around the lid of the jar.

1 cup granulated sugar

1 cup white wine vinegar

2 bay leaves

10 dried juniper berries

5 cloves

12 eggs, hard-boiled

1 large beet, cut into 1-inch pieces

✦ BEHIND THE MAGIC ✦

Gnarlak passes on the Ashwinder egg after spotting Newt's Bowtruckle, Pickett. (Bowtruckles can pick locks.)

In a medium saucepan over medium-high heat, combine the sugar, vinegar, 1 cup water, bay leaves, juniper berries, and cloves. Bring to a boil, and then reduce the heat to medium.

Place the eggs and beets in a large bowl or in canning jars. Pour the liquid mixture over the eggs and beets. Cover the eggs, and let them pickle in the mixture for at least 1 day; keep them refrigerated.

Slice each egg into quarters, and serve the pieces of egg on a plate mixed with the Salade Niçoise Teatime Boat Bites (page 80), Durmstrang Institute Shopska Salad Tea Party Boats (page 77), Ron Weasley's Finger Sandwich Bites (page 83), Aunt Petunia's Teatime Ham Bites (page 110), or Tina Goldstein's Bite-Size Hot Dogs with Honey Mustard Sauce (page 112). Or, give each guest 2 or 3 eggs in a canning jar to take home with them.

Store in the refrigerator in an airtight container for 1 to 2 months.

DEMENTORS MINI CHOCOLATE TEATIME TREATS

According to Professor Remus Lupin, Dementors feed on every good feeling and every happy memory a person has. They greatly affect Harry Potter upon their first appearance in *Harry Potter and the Prisoner of Azkaban*, as he had few happy childhood memories until he came to Hogwarts.

Prisoner of Azkaban director Alfonso Cuarón wanted the Dementors to have a completely different quality from other creatures seen onscreen, and one way to achieve this was with their very slow motions. He instructed the digital artists that Dementors are not in any hurry, and should move like royalty, describing them as "a force you cannot stop. And I think we created truly scary creatures," he adds.

Crunchy and coconutty, these Dementors have a chocolatey *goodness* that will only generate happy memories.

1 cup coconut

Two 12-ounce bags chocolate chips

2 tablespoons butter, softened

10 ounces dry chow mein noodles

1 tablespoon coarse salt flakes

NOTE ✦ For a vegan option, use dairy-free chocolate chips and butter.

Preheat the oven to 350°F. Line a baking sheet with parchment paper.

Place the coconut on the prepared baking sheet. Bake until lightly browned, about 8 minutes; stir after about 3 minutes. Remove from the oven, and set aside.

Place the chocolate chips and butter in a medium microwave-safe mixing bowl. Melt the chocolate chips in the microwave, stirring about every 20 seconds, just until the chocolate is completely melted.

Add the chow mein noodles and the toasted coconut to the melted chocolate. Stir to combine, making sure that every chow mein noodle is generously covered in chocolate.

✦ BEHIND THE MAGIC ✦

One way to defend against these cheerless, gloomy creatures is to cast *Expecto Patronum*—a spell that creates a positive force the Dementor feeds upon instead of the caster.

Place a 12-inch piece of waxed paper on the counter. Use an ice-cream scoop to form balls with the chocolate coated chow mein noodles. Place the balls on the waxed paper. Sprinkle coarse salt flakes over the top of each ball. Let the balls dry for about 1 hour or longer. When dry, arrange the balls on a serving platter. Create a platter with a mix of the Divination Dream Bar Tea Treats (page 20), Feverless Fudge Tea Bites (page 129), Dumbledore's Elderberry Tea Pastilles (page 143), Froggy Fancies (page 127), Disenchantment Tea Candies (page 133), or Chocolate Flying Keys (page 139).

Store at room temperature in an airtight container for 2 to 3 weeks.

> "DEMENTOR!
> DEMENTOR!"
>
> —Draco Malfoy trying
> to upset Harry Potter
>
> *Harry Potter and the
> Prisoner of Azkaban*

CHOCOLATE FLYING KEYS

In *Harry Potter and the Sorcerer's Stone*, Harry, Hermione, and Ron are challenged three times after they drop through a trapdoor in their search of the film's titular artifact. Hermione helps when they become entangled in Devil's Snare. Ron plays the "best played game of chess that Hogwarts has seen these many years," to quote Headmaster Dumbledore. And Harry uses his incredible talents on a broomstick to catch a winged key that will allow them access to the final challenge.

The digitally created keys were designed to be scary and wild—if they were beautiful, they would lose their threat to the young wizards. Their movement was also an important factor, and it was decided the keys would move in concert like a flock of birds, swirling and shooting around Harry as he flies around the room to catch the right key.

These one- or two-bite chocolate keys have a sweet raspberry flavor that helps counteract the bitterness of melted chocolate, giving them a fruity lightness and raising them to a new level. They'll fly off the plate!

2 cups chocolate chips

1 tablespoon raspberry extract

14 edible wings

SPECIALTY TOOLS

1 plastic key-shaped candy mold

Cooking spray

NOTE ✦ For a vegan option, use dairy-free chocolate chips.

In a double boiler over medium-low heat, or in a microwave-safe bowl in the microwave, melt the chocolate. If using the microwave, microwave for 1 minute, stirring after 30 seconds. Add the raspberry extract, and stir well. The mixture will become stiff, like the consistency of cookie dough.

Spray cooking spray inside the key-shaped molds. Wipe away excess with a soft cloth.

Using your fingers, place the chocolate mixture in the key molds. Spread the chocolate throughout each of the molds, ensuring the chocolate is the same thickness all over. Press in around the edges so that all of the chocolate is inside the mold. Push down on top of each mold that is filled with chocolate to flatten and smooth out the tops.

CONTINUED ON PAGE 140

CONTINUED FROM PAGE 140

Place the molds in the refrigerator until the chocolate is firm enough to remove it from the molds without breaking, about 4 hours.

Once set, carefully pull the chocolate from the molds.

Press a hot butter knife into the sides of each key at the top, and press an edible wing in on each side.

Tie a string ribbon around the handle of each key and hang the keys in a doorway, fireplace mantel, or window frame.

Store at room temperature in an airtight container for 2 to 3 weeks.

HONEYDUKES TAKE-HOME LOLLIPOPS

When Harry Potter finally makes his way to Honeydukes sweetshop in Hogsmeade (via the Marauder's Map as he cannot get his permission slip signed), he wears his Invisibility Cloak. Making his way through the shop, he "lifts" a shiny red lollipop from Neville Longbottom just as he's about to take a lick!

As seen in *Harry Potter and the Prisoner of Azkaban*, Honeydukes is packed with tall glass jars filled with sweets set in front of mint-green walls with cotton-candy-colored shelf accents. In addition to the candy, two displays feature eye-popping automatons. A top-hatted skeleton dispenses Eyeball Bonanza jawbreakers that are collected through his toothy mouth. The other is a bearded man tangling with house-elves who pull his hair. He dispenses strings of licorice from his beard.

Neville was enjoying a "blood pop" before Harry grabbed it upon his exit. These bright red lollipops are raspberry flavored. Place them on a tea tray by the door where guests can pick one up to take home.

Cooking spray

1½ cups granulated sugar

⅔ cup corn syrup

½ teaspoon cream of tartar

2 teaspoons raspberry extract

10 drops red food coloring

SPECIALTY TOOLS

Candy thermometer

1 sheet of lollipop candy molds with 10 molds on the sheet

Ten 2-inch-long lollipop sticks (these come with many lollipop molds)

Spray the lollipop molds with cooking spray. Set the mold on a baking sheet.

In a large saucepan over medium heat, combine the sugar, ¾ cup water, corn syrup, and cream of tartar. Bring the mixture to a boil; continue to cook until the temperature reaches 300°F on a candy thermometer. Remove from the heat, and stir in the raspberry extract and the food coloring until the coloring is completely blended into the mixture and there are no streaks.

Use a large spoon to put 1 teaspoon of the mixture into each of the cavities of the lollipop candy mold. Insert a stick into each of the molds, ensuring that ⅔ of the stick extends outside of the lollipop. Let the lollipop mold rest on the countertop until the lollipops are completely hardened, about 45 minutes. Pull each lollipop out of its mold, and wrap a 2-inch-square piece of plastic wrap around the lollipop. Twist the ends of the plastic wrap around the lollipop stick to close the plastic around the lollipop.

Store at room temperature in an airtight container for 3 to 5 weeks.

DUMBLEDORE'S ELDERBERRY TEA PASTILLES

Albus Dumbledore has a well-known affection for candy. After all, the password to enter the winding staircase to his office is "Sherbet Lemon." And he keeps a bowl of bite-happy Licorice Snaps on his desk. He would probably love these sweet teatime treats—and one reason could be in the name. After all, he wields the Elder Wand!

The props department was tasked with creating all the candies, pastries, and other confections that appear at sweetshops such as Honeydukes. Thousands of silicone candies were molded for Weasleys' Wizard Wheezes. And for the wedding of Bill Weasley and Fleur Delacour in *Harry Potter and the Deathly Hallows – Part 1*, four thousand small cakes, petits fours, and other bite-size confectioneries were crafted (along with a four-tiered cake).

These entrancing candies are made with elderberry jam in the form of a pastille—a small treat meant to melt in your mouth.

1 cup elderberry jam

1 tablespoon honey

2 tablespoons unflavored gelatin

½ cup granulated sugar

1 tablespoon butter

1 cup powdered sugar

"OH, HARRY, DO FEEL FREE TO INDULGE IN A LITTLE LICORICE SNAP IN MY ABSENCE. BUT I HAVE TO WARN YOU, THEY'RE A WEE BIT SHARP."

—Albus Dumbledore

Harry Potter and the Goblet of Fire

Line a small baking dish with parchment paper, being careful to line the sides of the dish.

In a medium saucepan over high heat, combine the jam, honey, gelatin, granulated sugar, and butter, and bring to a boil. Boil for 4 minutes, stirring continuously. The mixture will become thick.

Pour the mixture into the prepared baking dish. Let sit until the mixture is formed and becomes thick enough that a knife is needed to cut it, at least 4 hours.

Use a knife to cut the candies, in the dish, into 1-inch rectangles or squares.

Place the powdered sugar in a medium bowl. Remove the candies from the dish where they formed and add the 1-inch pieces to the powdered sugar. Toss the candies in the sugar until they are coated all around. Let the candies sit in an airtight container overnight in the refrigerator. Arrange the candies on a small plate to serve them.

Store in the refrigerator in an airtight container for 1 to 2 weeks. Remove the candies from the refrigerator 1 hour before serving so they can be served at room temperature.

CHAPTER FOUR

TEATIME TIPPLES, HOT DRINKS, AND MAGICAL MIXES

HOGWARTS HOUSE TEAS

House pride at Hogwarts means displaying your house colors, whether it's on your robes or on banners cheering on your house Quidditch team. There's a very special item in Hogwarts' Great Hall that showcases the house colors: the house points hourglasses set behind the professors' high table. House points are gained or lost by students, culminating in the awarding of the House Cup at the end of the school year. The hourglasses were fully functional, and careful attention was paid to place the beads at the top compartment at the beginning of each school year, as no points had been won yet.

This selection of teas represents each of the Hogwarts houses in color and flavor. The rosy red of geraniums evokes Gryffindor red. A ginger tea with honey suggests the yellow of Hufflepuff; butterfly pea flower conjures up the Ravenclaw blue. And a lemony green mint tea represents Slytherin house.

These house-colorful teas would perfectly accompany the Hogwarts Houses Four-Layer Rainbow Petits Fours (page 65)!

FOR THE HONEYED GINGER HUFFLEPUFF TEA

- 1 tablespoon chopped fresh ginger
- ¼ teaspoon clover honey
- 5 drops yellow food coloring

BUTTERFLY PEA FLOWER RAVENCLAW TEA

- 1 tablespoon crushed dried butterfly pea flowers
- ¼ teaspoon lemon juice
- ¼ teaspoon honey

TO MAKE THE HONEYED GINGER HUFFLEPUFF TEA

Fill a teacup with hot water. Place the ginger in a tea infuser, and add it to the hot water. Steep for 2 minutes. Add the honey and yellow food coloring and stir 3 revolutions with a spoon.

TO MAKE THE BUTTERFLY PEA FLOWER RAVENCLAW TEA

Fill a teacup with hot water. Place the dried butterfly pea flowers in a tea infuser and place the infuser in the hot water. Steep the tea for 1 minute. Add the lemon and honey, and stir to combine.

CONTINUED ON PAGE 149

CONTINUED FROM PAGE 147

FOR THE LEMONY MINT SLYTHERIN TEA

1 tablespoon chopped fresh mint leaves

½ thin slice fresh lemon

1 drop green food coloring

FOR THE STRAWBERRY-SCENTED GERANIUM GRYFFINDOR TEA

1 tablespoon crushed dried scented geranium leaves

1 drop red food coloring

1 fresh scented geranium leaf

3 freeze-dried strawberry slices

TO MAKE THE LEMONY MINT SLYTHERIN TEA

Fill a teacup with hot water. Place the mint in a tea infuser, and add the infuser to the hot water. Steep for 2 minutes. Add the fresh lemon and the green food coloring; stir.

TO MAKE THE STRAWBERRY-SCENTED GERANIUM GRYFFINDOR TEA

Fill a teacup with hot water. Place the dried geranium leaves in a tea infuser. Place the tea infuser in the hot water. Steep for 1 minute.

Remove the tea infuser, and add the red food coloring. Stir the color into the tea until well blended.

Garnish with 1 fresh scented geranium leaf and the freeze-dried strawberry slices.

✦ BEHIND THE MAGIC ✦

Tens of thousands of glass beads were used in the house points hourglasses, which caused a shortage of beads in Britain!

GF, V, V+
YIELD: 1 SERVING

GINGER WITCH WHISKEY SOUR

Whiskey sours were popular cocktails in New York City in the 1930s, and this gingery version, inspired by a unique, unseen character in the wizarding world, will be popular among your royal tea guests, with a perfect blend of sweet and sour.

To fill the columns of *The Daily Prophet*, graphic designers Miraphora Mina and Eduardo Lima wrote titles about Quidditch matches, author appearances, and contest winners. There has also been one reoccurring character called the "Ginger Witch" who has had a career as a criminal from the 1920s to at least the 1990s. Her first appearance is in *Harry Potter and the Prisoner of Azkaban*, but her hooliganism dates back to the days of *Fantastic Beasts and Where to Find Them*.

FOR THE GINGER SIMPLE SYRUP

- ½ cup granulated sugar
- 1 tablespoon chopped fresh ginger

FOR THE COCKTAIL

- 2 fluid ounces Scotch whisky
- 1 fluid ounce fresh lemon juice

FOR THE GARNISH

- ½ thin slice fresh lemon
- 1 maraschino cherry

TO MAKE THE GINGER SIMPLE SYRUP

In a small saucepan over high heat, bring the sugar, ½ cup water, and ginger to a boil. Stir continuously, and boil until the sugar is completely dissolved. Reduce the heat to medium, and let the mixture simmer for 30 minutes. Remove from the heat, and set aside to cool to room temperature. Strain the ginger from the liquid by pouring the liquid through a handheld fine-mesh strainer into a large bowl.

TO MAKE THE COCKTAIL

Fill a coupe glass ⅔ full with ice; add the whisky, ¼ of the ginger simple syrup, and lemon juice, and stir well.

Garnish with the lemon slice and cherry on a bamboo cocktail pick.

Use the extra ginger simple syrup for flavoring teas, cocktails, and desserts. Store in the refrigerator in an airtight container for 2 to 3 days.

✦ BEHIND THE MAGIC ✦

Throughout her notorious career, the Ginger Witch has been prosecuted for wig theft, implicated in a product recall of Bertie Bott's Every Flavour Beans, and was arrested at a Muggle football match.

"MYSTERIOUS GINGER WITCH UNDER INVESTIGATION"

—*The Daily Prophet*, November 1926

Fantastic Beasts and Where to Find Them

TEDDY THE NIFFLER'S MILK TREAT

Teddy the Niffler, who stole our hearts in *Fantastic Beasts and Where to Find Them*, becomes a bit of a scamp in *Fantastic Beasts: The Crimes of Grindelwald*, though his thieving ways prove vital to helping Dumbledore defeat Grindelwald. Teddy was able to swipe the vial that contains their blood oath to never fight each other.

Inspirations for the Niffler's amusing look and spirited character came from moles, platypuses, and echidnas. Video references of these animals using their paws were studied. "We also found great footage of a honey badger ransacking somebody's house," says visual effects supervisor Christian Manz. "It was just an insatiable desire for food, going through fridges and cupboards. Those real-world animalistic traits went into the Niffler, which is why I think he's so successful."

This malted milk treat with fresh whipped cream would be a worthy reward for Teddy's actions in stealing the vial. Chocolate sprinkles on top pay tribute to the Niffler's spiky black fur.

FOR THE MALTED MILK DRINK

2 tablespoons chocolate syrup

1 tablespoon chocolate sprinkles (see note)

1 cup whole milk

½ cup malted milk powder

FOR THE WHIPPED CREAM TOPPING

½ cup heavy whipping cream

1 teaspoon granulated sugar

½ teaspoon lemon juice

NOTE ✦ Use ¼-inch-long dark brown chocolate sprinkles that look like Niffler's whiskers.

TO MAKE THE MALTED MILK DRINK

Place the chocolate syrup on a plate, and dip the rim of a clear glass into the chocolate. Swirl the rim around in a circular motion to ensure that the entire rim is coated with the chocolate syrup.

Place the chocolate sprinkles on a separate large plate. Place the rim of the glass into the sprinkles, and roll the rim around to ensure that sprinkles coat the entire rim of the glass.

In a mixing glass, use a barspoon to mix the milk with the malted milk powder. Stir briskly until the powder dissolves and the milk and powder are combined well, about 2 minutes.

TO MAKE THE WHIPPED CREAM TOPPING

In the bowl of a stand mixer or a large mixing bowl with a hand mixer, beat the heavy whipping cream, sugar, and lemon juice together on low until well combined and starting to thicken so it won't splatter, about 3 minutes. Increase the speed to high and beat the cream until thickened enough to form soft peaks, 12 to 15 minutes.

Pour the drink into the clear glass, and top with 2 tablespoons of the whipped cream topping.

Store in the refrigerator in an airtight container for 1 to 2 days.

TREVOR'S TOAD POND PUNCH

Neville Longbottom brings a toad with him to his first year at Hogwarts and loses him—twice—in *Harry Potter and the Sorcerer's Stone*. Four toads shared the role of Trevor, Neville's often-misplaced companion.

The real name of the toad most frequently onscreen was, coincidentally, Harry. However, this Harry did not enjoy being held and would try to jump out of Matthew Lewis's (Neville's) hands into his face or onto other actors.

In spite of this, Lewis did enjoy the humor Trevor brought to the story and would definitely raise a glass to him of this lemon-lime and green apple drink that fizzes with the addition of sherbet. Serve this frothy treat in a large punch bowl as your substitute "toad pond," or in individual clear, stemmed wine or coupe glasses.

2 liters lemon-lime soda, chilled

½ cup green apple–flavored drink powder

6 cups ice

1½ quarts lemon or lime sherbet

SPECIALTY TOOLS

Clear glass punch bowl and ladle

In a pitcher or a punch bowl, combine the soda and drink powder. Mix together until the drink powder is completely dissolved, 3 to 5 minutes.

Add the ice. Add spoonfuls of the sherbet all around the punch bowl and in the center.

Serve these with Divination Dream Bar Tea Treats (page 20) that have been cut into the shapes of lily pads using a flower-shaped or a lily pad–shaped cookie cutter.

Store in the refrigerator in an airtight container for 1 to 2 days.

ALBUS DUMBLEDORE'S APPLE BUTTER AND BRANDY HOT TODDY

GF, V, V+ ✦ YIELD: 1
DRINK; 4 SERVINGS
APPLE BUTTER

In *Harry Potter and the Prisoner of Azkaban*, Harry and Hermione use her Time-Turner to save Hagrid's Hippogriff, Buckbeak, by leading him away and hiding him after the creature had been sentenced for execution. Once it's learned that Buckbeak is nowhere to be found, the executioner is dismissed, and Albus Dumbledore gestures for Minister for Magic Cornelius Fudge to join him in Hagrid's hut for a cup of tea, or better yet, a brandy.

"We talked about having the Hippogriff sitting down in the pumpkin patch," says creature effects supervisor Nick Dudman. "And I said, 'We can do that.' It would be attached to a chain the kids will tug on. I said we could do that, too. And then they said Buckbeak would get up and walk away with them. And I said, 'Ah, no. I don't think we can do that!'"

On days like the cold, rainy ones over which this sequence was shot, this apple-buttery hot drink spiced with cinnamon and mint would have been greatly appreciated by the cast and crew.

FOR THE APPLE BUTTER

- 2 large honeycrisp apples, peeled and cut into 1-inch pieces
- 2 tablespoons brown sugar
- Juice of 1 lemon
- 1 teaspoon ground cinnamon
- ¼ teaspoon grated nutmeg

FOR THE DRINK

- 2 fluid ounces brandy
- 2 ounces hot water
- ½ teaspoon fresh lemon juice

FOR THE GARNISH

- 2 thin slices fresh honeycrisp apple
- 2 large mint leaves
- 1 cinnamon stick

TO MAKE THE APPLE BUTTER

In a small saucepan over high heat, combine the apples, 1 cup water, brown sugar, lemon juice, cinnamon, and nutmeg. Bring the mixture to a boil, stirring continuously, until thickened, about 4 minutes. Reduce the heat to medium, and simmer for 40 minutes.

Store in the refrigerator in an airtight container for 4 to to 5 days.

TO MAKE THE DRINK

Pour the brandy in a clear glass mug; add the hot water and the lemon juice. Stir, and add 1 tablespoon of the apple butter. Stir rapidly.

Garnish with 2 very thin slices of fresh apple and 2 large mint leaves on a cocktail pick; add the cinnamon stick as a stirrer.

> "WELL SEARCH THE SKIES IF YOU MUST. MINISTER. MEANWHILE. I'D LIKE A NICE CUP OF TEA OR A LARGE BRANDY."
>
> —Albus Dumbledore
>
> *Harry Potter and the Prisoner of Azkaban*

PROFESSOR TRELAWNEY'S DIVINATION TEA

Professor Sybill Trelawney's first lesson for her Divination class in *Harry Potter and the Prisoner of Azkaban* is the art of reading tea leaves, where each student reads the cup of the person sitting opposite them. Ron reads Harry's and interprets the shapes of the tea leaves as being Harry will suffer but be happy about it. When Trelawney looks into Harry's cup, she sees the Grim, a giant spectral dog that is an omen of death.

This drink features linden leaves, which not only make for a great-tasting tea, but they also have been used throughout history for divination purposes. Dreaming of a linden tree itself portends good news in the future! Once you've drunk the tea, you might want to try your own hand at tessomancy with the leftover leaves.

20 large dried linden tree leaves

One ½-inch lemon slice

Use a mortar and pestle to crush the linden tree leaves into a fine, sandy consistency, about 5 minutes. Place the crushed tree leaves into a tea infuser. Fill a teacup ¾ full with hot water. Add the infuser, and stir. Add the lemon.

After the tea has been consumed, study the pattern of the remaining tea sediment.

✦ BEHIND THE MAGIC ✦

"I think she has a genuine gift," says actress Emma Thompson of Trelawney. "But like all those [who do this], she has to make it stretch. She has to make it bigger than it actually is." Trelawney's predictions have a tendency toward gloom and doom, which Thompson believes helps to "ratchet things up."

"THIS TERM WE SHALL BE FOCUSING ON TESSOMANCY, WHICH IS THE ART OF READING TEA LEAVES. SO PLEASE, TAKE THE CUP OF THE PERSON SITTING OPPOSITE YOU."

—Sybill Trelawney

Harry Potter and the Prisoner of Azkaban

GOLDSTEIN SISTERS' COINTREAU HOT CHOCOLATE

While staying at the Goldstein sisters' apartment in *Fantastic Beasts and Where to Find Them*, Tina offers Newt and Jacob hot cocoa as a soothing bedtime treat. Jacob tries to get Newt to join him, but the Magizoologist seems to be asleep. However, once Tina leaves, Newt jumps out of bed and descends inside his case, beckoning for an amazed Jacob to follow him. The No-Maj is enchanted at the magical creatures inside.

Building upon Tina's chocolate beverage, for this drink, each guest's teacup has a shot of Cointreau, an orange-flavored liqueur, and a chocolate ball filled with mini marshmallows and edible gold glitter. After the host pours hot milk over the chocolate ball, guests stir rapidly until the chocolate ball melts into the steamy milk, releasing the marshmallows and edible gold glitter. Royal tea guests will surely be as spellbound as Jacob was with Tina's cocoa as they enjoy the hot chocolate "magic" of this delightful drink.

¼ cup chocolate chips

1 teaspoon butter

5 mini marshmallows

¼ teaspoon edible gold luster dust and glitter

1 cup whole milk

1 tablespoon Cointreau

1 teaspoon orange zest

SPECIALTY TOOLS

1 sheet of plastic candy molds to make 2-inch hollow chocolate balls

NOTE ✦ For a vegan option, make this with hot water in place of hot milk and use carob chips in place of milk chocolate chips.

In a large microwave-safe bowl in the microwave or in a double boiler over medium heat, melt the chocolate and butter just until the chips are all completely melted and the butter and chocolate are blended together thoroughly. If melting the chocolate in the microwave, heat the chocolate on medium for 1 minute, stir, and heat for another minute.

Using a pastry brush, coat the inside of each of the halves of the ball mold evenly with the chocolate. Pull the chocolate up along the sides to the top edge of the ball mold all around. Repeat this multiple times all around, until the inside of each mold is covered about ¼ inch thick with chocolate. Use a clean butter knife to go around the edge of the molds, evening out the chocolate around the edges.

Place the mold in the refrigerator until the chocolate hardens enough to stand on its own once the mold is removed, 10 to 15 minutes.

When the chocolate has set, remove the mold from the refrigerator, and pull the chocolate ball away from the mold. Using a pastry brush, go around the edge of the top and bottom halves of the mold with hot water so that the chocolate softens just enough so that both the top and bottom halves of the mold will stick when they are brought together.

Place 5 mini marshmallows and ¼ teaspoon edible gold dust in the center of one of the halves of the chocolate ball. Bring the halves of the ball together so that the edges line up, and lightly press until the halves are secured together, about 3 minutes. Place the ball in the refrigerator to harden together well, about 3 minutes.

In a small saucepan over high heat, bring the milk to a boil. Reduce the heat to medium-low, and simmer the milk until it is time to pour it.

Pour 1 tablespoon of Cointreau in a mug, and place a chocolate ball in the mug.

Put the hot milk in a teapot, and pour the hot milk into the mug.

Garnish with orange zest.

Stir rapidly to help along the release of the glitter, marshmallow, and chocolate as the chocolate melts under the heat of the milk. Stir continually until milk and chocolate are combined well.

"I THOUGHT YOU MIGHT LIKE A HOT DRINK?"

—Tina Goldstein

Fantastic Beasts and Where to Find Them

+ BEHIND THE MAGIC +

The bottom of Newt's case and the floor below it were removed for his descent. Then a ladder was placed inside for Eddie Redmayne to disappear down. Dan Fogler's character, Jacob, was a tighter fit trying to get into the case. Jacob gets himself inside with a few "jumps"—a bit of digital movie magic.

THE NEW YORK GHOST WAKE-UP CALL DRAMBUIE BREW

GF, V, V+*
YIELD: 2 SERVINGS

The New York Ghost, the local wizarding newspaper in *Fantastic Beasts and Where to Find Them*, advertises a robust caffeine-type drink called "Wakey-Up Brew." The wizarding world's java pick-me-up may be rivaled in getting your get-up-and-go going by this very strong, anise-flavored coffee drink, flavored with Drambuie, a special Scotch whisky. It's a dynamic addition to any royal tea.

The graphics department was tasked with creating the many newspapers published in the wizarding world since *The Daily Prophet* in the Harry Potter films. They also came up with ideas for the advertisements and article titles that peppered the papers. In order to give the paper that worn newsprint look, the pages would be dipped into a special coffee blend, then laid out on the floor in the hallways to dry. Due to this, every newspaper seen in the wizarding world films has a slight coffee smell to it.

FOR THE WHIPPED CREAM

½ pint heavy whipping cream

1 teaspoon granulated sugar

Juice of ¼ fresh lemon

FOR THE DRAMBUIE COFFEE

1 cup ice

4 fluid ounces Drambuie

2 cups brewed coffee, cooled to room temperature

FOR THE GARNISH

2 sprigs fresh mint

1 pinch edible gold luster dust and sparkles

NOTE ✦ To make a vegan option, replace the whipped cream with a nondairy creamer.

TO MAKE THE WHIPPED CREAM

In the bowl of a stand mixer or a large mixing bowl with a hand mixer, beat the whipping cream, granulated sugar, and lemon juice together on low until well combined and starting to thicken so it won't splatter, about 3 minutes. Increase the speed to high and beat the cream until thickened enough to form soft peaks, 12 to 15 minutes.

TO MAKE THE DRAMBUIE COFFEE

Fill 2 clear glass coffee mugs with ½ cup ice. Pour 2 fluid ounces of the Drambuie over the ice in each glass, followed by 1 cup of the coffee. Top each glass with the whipped cream.

Garnish with a sprig of fresh mint and edible gold luster dust and sparkles.

> "POSSIBLY MORE POTENT THAN NO-MAJ COFFEE!"
>
> —Advertisement in *The New York Ghost* for Wakey-Up Brew
>
> *Fantastic Beasts and Where to Find Them*

"YOU'RE GOING TO BE
DOING SOME LINES
FOR ME TODAY, MR.
POTTER. NO, NOT WITH
YOUR QUILL. YOU'RE
GOING TO BE USING A
RATHER SPECIAL ONE
OF MINE."

—Dolores Umbridge

*Harry Potter and the
Order of the Phoenix*

PROFESSOR UMBRIDGE'S EARL GREY TEA AND RASPBERRY CHAMPAGNE COCKTAIL

Before Dolores Umbridge supervises Harry at his detention in her office, in *Harry Potter and the Order of the Phoenix*, she makes herself a cup of tea, stirring in at least three teaspoons of pink sugar. However, she does not seem to stir her tea correctly according to teatime "rules"—she stirs it in a circle instead of back and forth—but she does hold her cup correctly, with a firm grasp on the handle, no pinky askew.

Regarding Harry's detention, "[Umbridge] thinks that's perfectly fair," says Imelda Staunton. However, the actress found it alarming that Umbridge uses punishment as a way of teaching, and stated that she felt terrible after filming the scene.

This royal tea tipple is inspired by the tea service and pink colors in scenes featuring Professor Umbridge. For a nonalcoholic option, you can make these with lemon-lime soda in place of champagne.

1 ice cube	Place the ice cube into a champagne or wineglass.
1 cup champagne or sparkling wine, chilled	In a mixing glass, combine the champagne and tea, and stir.
1 tablespoon brewed, steeped Earl Grey tea, room temperature	In a separate glass or in a bowl, use the back of a large spoon to muddle the sugar and 3 raspberries, and add this to the mixing glass.
½ teaspoon granulated sugar	Stir the ingredients together until well blended, about 15 revolutions with a barspoon.
4 fresh raspberries, divided	Pour the mixture over the ice. Garnish with the remaining raspberry set on a bamboo cocktail pick; rest it across the rim of the glass.

"I'VE BEEN STUDYING HIM. AND I'M PRETTY SURE HIS VENOM COULD BE QUITE USEFUL IF PROPERLY DILUTED. JUST TO REMOVE BAD MEMORIES, YOU KNOW."

—Newt Scamander

Fantastic Beasts and Where to Find Them

SWOOPING EVIL BLUEBERRY AND MINT AVIATION COCKTAIL

Newt Scamander's been traveling the world, rescuing, rehabilitating, and learning as much as he can about magical creatures, including one the locals call the Swooping Evil—"not the friendliest of names," Newt says. Through his knowledge, Newt knows he can use the venom from the Swooping Evil to Obliviate the memory of 1927 New York City's residents after the destruction caused by the Obscurial Credence Barebone. The venom is distributed by a Thunderbird, another creature Newt rescued, who creates a rainstorm that disperses the contents of a blue-colored vial.

The creature designers referenced both butterflies and bats for the Swooping Evil, whose underside is colored a rich cobalt blue. Its head resembles that of a rodent, with sharp, saber-shaped teeth. However "evil" it looks, it is only helpful to Newt and his friends.

This Swooping Evil cocktail, perfect for a royal tea, is a refreshing, minty spin on the classic aviation cocktail. A hint of blueberry balances out the violet flavor.

3 plump blueberries, divided

1 large sprig fresh mint

1 cup ice

2 fluid ounces gin

¼ fluid ounce crème de violette

½ fluid ounce fresh lemon juice

1 pinch lemon zest

1 pinch edible gold luster dust and tiny stars

Muddle 1 blueberry and 3 mint leaves by grinding them together using a mortar and pestle. In place of a mortar and pestle, mash the ingredients in a small bowl, using a spoon.

In a cocktail shaker, combine the ice, gin, crème de violette, lemon juice, and the muddled blueberry and mint. Shake for 20 revolutions.

Strain into a coupe glass. Place the remaining 2 blueberries and a large sprig of fresh mint on a bamboo cocktail pick, and place across the rim of the glass as a garnish. Sprinkle the top with lemon zest and the edible gold luster dust.

✦ MUGGLE MAGIC ✦

The aviation cocktail was invented in New York City in the early twentieth century. Its name comes from the sky-blue color that results from the use of crème de violette in a nod to a time when air travel was still a new and glamorous form of transportation.

PROFESSOR SNAPE'S BLUEBERRY-SAGE SPRITZER

Professor Severus Snape is a very "buttoned-up" type of wizard, very reserved and not inclined to reveal his thoughts. He's also "buttoned up" literally—buttons run up to his neck, up his long sleeves, and even on his pants over his boots.

This magical mix was inspired by Snape's blue robes, which photographed black on film, and the idea that maybe, in a moment of relaxation, he would set his mind to creating a refreshing, energizing beverage instead of a potion. For a royal tea option, substitute sparkling wine for the sparkling water.

Buttons were one of the stipulations Alan Rickman requested when his costume was designed. Rickman knew his costume was an important indication of the very focused life that Snape led. "You know he lives a solitary existence; you're not quite sure what the details of that are. He doesn't have much of a social life, and clearly, he's only got one set of clothes!" he said.

½ cup fresh
  blueberries, divided

1 teaspoon coarse sugar
  crystals

1 teaspoon fresh sage
  leaves, chopped, plus
  3 whole fresh leaves,
  divided

1 cup sparkling water

NOTE ✦ This is a
refreshing nonalcoholic
drink, but you can replace
the sparkling water with
sparkling wine for a more
intoxicating option.

Using a mortar and pestle, muddle together ¼ cup blueberries, the sugar, and 1 teaspoon fresh chopped sage leaves.

Fill a large clear glass half full with ice. Place the blueberry sage mixture and the remaining ¼ cup blueberries into the glass, followed by the sparkling water. Stir this together well. Add 3 sage leaves as garnish.

"I CAN TEACH YOU HOW TO BEWITCH THE MIND
AND ENSNARE THE SENSES."

—Severus Snape to his first-years' Potions class

Harry Potter and the Sorcerer's Stone

DIETARY CONSIDERATIONS

SWEET FINGER TREATS AND SUGARY NIBBLES

Hagrid's Pumpkin Teatime Madeleines ✦ V

Jacob Kowalski's Mini Teatime Paczki ✦ V

Nicolas Flamel's French Fancies ✦ V

Hogwarts High Table Roasted Apple Scone Bites with Fresh Cream and Mint ✦ V

Divination Dream Bar Tea Treats ✦ V

Aunt Petunia's Teatime Windtorte Pudding ✦ GF, V

Hungarian Horntail Mini Tea Puddings ✦ V

Professor Umbridge's Load of Waffles ✦ V

Paris Pâtisserie Two-Bite Lavender Teatime Canelés ✦ V

Professor McGonagall's Transfigurational Sticky Toffee Pudding Bites ✦ V

Molly Weasley's Individual Teatime Rhubarb and Custard Trifles ✦ V

Professor Slughorn's One-Bite High Tea Profiteroles ✦ V

Kowalski Bakery's Occamy Egg Teatime Surprise ✦ GF, V

Honeydukes Lemon Drop Meringue Teatime Bites ✦ V

One-Bite Circus Animal Tea Biscuits ✦ V

Queenie's Mini Brandied Apple Strudels with Apple Mint Sauce ✦ GF, V

Professor Sprout's Bite-Size Greenhouse Mystery Cakes ✦ V

Place Cachée Orange-Scented Teatime Pastry Puffs ✦ V

Hogwarts Houses Four-Layer Rainbow Petits Fours ✦ V

Dolores Umbridge's I Will Make Scones

Teddy the Niffler's Two-Bite Gold Coin Pudding Sandwiches ✦ V

Queenie Goldstein's Floating Teapot ✦ GF, V

SAVORY TEATIME FINGER FOODS

Durmstrang Institute Shopska Salad Tea Party Boats ✦ GF, V

Mini Fried Raven Egg Tea Sandwiches ✦ GF

Salade Niçoise Teatime Boat Bites ✦ GF

Ron Weasley's Finger Sandwich Bites

Leaky Cauldron Split Pea Teatime Soup ✦ GF

Forbidden Forest Mini Mushroom Strudels ✦ V

Luna Lovegood's Honey-Roasted Radish Salad ✦ GF, V

Black Lake Cod Cakes with Poached Eggs and Brandy Cream Sauce ✦ GF

Deathly Hallows Pull-Apart Teatime Bread ✦ V

Great Hall Treacle and Pinot Noir–Roasted Turkey Drumsticks ✦ GF

Bowtruckle Island Butter Board ✦ GF

"Good Gravy!" Mini Meat Loaf Tea Sandwiches

Ron Weasley's Teatime Raspberry Gelatin Treats ✦ GF

Hagrid's Butternut Squash Mini Tartlets with Crispy Bacon and Sage ✦ V

Aunt Petunia's Teatime Ham Bites

Tina Goldstein's Bite-Size Hot Dogs with Honey Mustard Sauce ✦ GF

Ron Weasley's Savory Escargot-Stuffed Mushrooms

Kowalski Bakery's Buttery Teatime Witch Hats with Magical Herbal Broomsticks ✦ V

Molly Weasley's Bangers and Roasted Tomato Quiche Bites

FRY STATION SAFETY TIPS

TEATIME CANDIES, SNACKS, AND TAKE-HOME GIFTS

Froggie Fancies ✦ GF, V, V+

Feverless Fudge Tea Bites ✦ GF, V

Grandfather Goldstein's Teatime Owl Food ✦ GF, V

Disenchantment Tea Candies ✦ GF, V

Pickled "Ashwinder" Eggs ✦ GF, V

Dementors Mini Chocolate Teatime Treats ✦ V, V+

Chocolate Flying Keys ✦ GF, V, V+

Honeydukes Take-Home Lollipops ✦ GF, V, V+

Dumbledore's Elderberry Tea Pastilles ✦ GF, V

TEATIME TIPPLES, HOT DRINKS, AND MAGICAL MIXES

Hogwarts House Teas ✦ GF, V

Ginger Witch Whiskey Sour ✦ GF, V, V+

Teddy the Niffler's Milk Treat ✦ GF, V

Trevor's Toad Pond Punch ✦ GF, V

Albus Dumbledore's Apple Butter and Brandy Hot Toddy ✦ GF, V, V+

Professor Trelawney's Divination Tea ✦ GF, V, V+

Goldstein Sisters' Cointreau Hot Chocolate ✦ V, V+

The New York Ghost Wake-Up Call Drambuie Brew ✦ GF, V, V+

Professor Umbridge's Earl Grey Tea and Raspberry Champagne Cocktail ✦ GF, V, V+

Swooping Evil Blueberry and Mint Aviation Cocktail ✦ GF, V, V+

Professor Snape's Blueberry-Sage Spritzer ✦ GF, V, V+

If you're making something that requires deep-frying, here are some important tips to keep you safe:

✦ If you don't have a dedicated deep-fryer, use a Dutch oven or a high-walled sauté pan.

✦ Never have too much oil in the pan! You don't want hot oil spilling out as soon as you put the food in.

✦ Use only a suitable cooking oil, such as canola, peanut, or vegetable oil.

✦ Always keep track of the oil temperature with a thermometer; 350° to 375°F should do the trick.

✦ Never put too much food in the pan at the same time!

✦ Never put wet food in the pan. It will splatter and can cause burns.

✦ Always have a lid nearby to cover the pan, in case it starts to spill over or catch fire. A properly rated fire extinguisher is also great to have on hand in case of emergencies.

✦ Never leave the pan unattended, and never let children near the pan.

✦ Never, ever put your face, your hand, or any other body part in the hot oil.

METRIC CONVERSTION CHART

KITCHEN MEASUREMENTS

CUPS	TABLESPOONS	TEASPOONS	FLUID OUNCES
⅟₁₆ cup	1 tbsp	3 tsp	½ fl oz
⅛ cup	2 tbsp	6 tsp	1 fl oz
¼ cup	4 tbsp	12 tsp	2 fl oz
⅓ cup	5½ tbsp	16 tsp	2⅔ fl oz
½ cup	8 tbsp	24 tsp	4 fl oz
⅔ cup	10⅔ tbsp	32 tsp	5⅓ fl oz
¾ cup	12 tbsp	36 tsp	6 fl oz
1 cup	16 tbsp	48 tsp	8 fl oz

GALLONS	QUARTS	PINTS	CUPS	FLUID OUNCES
⅟₁₆ gal	¼ qt	½ pt	1 cup	8 fl oz
⅛ gal	½ qt	1 pt	2 cups	16 fl oz
¼ gal	1 qt	2 pt	4 cups	32 fl oz
½ gal	2 qt	4 pt	8 cups	64 fl oz
1 gal	4 qt	8 pt	16 cups	128 fl oz

WEIGHT

GRAMS	OUNCES
14 g	½ oz
28 g	1 oz
57 g	2 oz
85 g	3 oz
113 g	4 oz
142 g	5 oz
170 g	6 oz
283 g	10 oz
397 g	14 oz
454 g	16 oz
907 g	32 oz

OVEN TEMPERATURES

FAHRENHEIT	CELSIUS
200 ˚F	93 ˚C
225 ˚F	107 ˚C
250 ˚F	121 ˚C
275 ˚F	135 ˚C
300 ˚F	149 ˚C
325 ˚F	163 ˚C
350 ˚F	177 ˚C
375 ˚F	191 ˚C
400 ˚F	204 ˚C
425 ˚F	218 ˚C
450 ˚F	232 ˚C

LENGTH

IMPERIAL	METRIC
1 in	2.5 cm
2 in	5 cm
4 in	10 cm
6 in	15 cm
8 in	20 cm
10 in	25 cm
12 in	30 cm

INDEX

INSIGHT
EDITIONS

PO Box 3088
San Rafael, CA 94912
www.insighteditions.com

Find us on Facebook: www.facebook.com/InsightEditions
Follow us on Instagram: @insighteditions

ISBN: 979-8-88663-160-9
Exclusive: 979-8-88663-659-8

Publisher: Raoul Goff
VP, Co-Publisher: Vanessa Lopez
VP, Creative: Chrissy Kwasnik
VP, Manufacturing: Alix Nicholaeff
VP, Group Managing Editor: Vicki Jaeger
Publishing Director: Jamie Thompson
Designer: Brooke McCullum
Senior Editor: Anna Wostenberg
Editorial Assistant: Sami Alvarado
Senior Production Editor: Nora Milman
Production Associate: Deena Hashem
Senior Production Manager, Subsidiary Rights: Lina s Palma-Temena

Photographer: Ted Thomas
Food and Prop Stylist: Elena P. Craig
Assistant Food Stylist: Patricia Parrish
Photoshoot Art Director: Judy Wiatrek Trum
Illustrations: Paula Hanback

ROOTS of PEACE   REPLANTED PAPER

Insight Editions, in association with Roots of Peace, will plant two trees for each
tree used in the manufacturing of this book. Roots of Peace is an internationally
renowned humanitarian organization dedicated to eradicating land mines
worldwide and converting war-torn lands into productive farms and wildlife
habitats. Roots of Peace will plant two million fruit and nut trees in Afghanistan
and provide farmers there with the skills and support necessary for sustainable
land use.

Manufactured in China by Insight Editions

10 9 8 7 6 5 4 3 2

CONCEPT ART

Page 8

Ron and Harry arrive at the
Weasley home, The Burrow, via a
flying car in Harry Potter and the
Chamber of Secrets in artwork by
Andrew Williamson.

Page 29

Concept art by Paul Catling
of the Hungarian Horntail,
Harry's dragon for the Triwizard
Tournament's first task in Harry
Potter and the Goblet of Fire.

Page 167

Studies of the Swooping Evil by
artist Dan Baker for Fantastic
Beasts and Where to Find Them
explored the terrifying creature
in its cocoon form and with its
wings fully open.